SUSTAINABLE ENGAGEMENT

Strategic Planning for **Positive** Social Change

William D. Gibson
with LaVerne Lewis

Cover photos: Christina Wocintechchat
Photos: Cited photographers from Unsplash.com

A Sustineri Group, Inc. Publication
ISBN 978-163877369–6
sustinerigroup.co

⫽BookBaby

Published and Distributed by BookBaby
bookbaby.com • Pennsauken, NJ 08110

Edited by LaVerne Lewis and Patrick Ferguson

SUSTAINABLE ENGAGEMENT
Strategic Planning for Positive Social Change
By William D. Gibson
with LaVerne Lewis
williamdgibson.com
wgibson@sustinerigroup.co
llewis@sustinerigroup.co

Table of Contents

Introduction

Many years ago, I had a conversation with my father. I told him about a new business idea that my former business partner and I were developing. My dad was not a business person. Instead, he was a meticulous technician, both in his professional life and personal projects. He was always interested in process and how things fit together. When I finished pitching our idea, he responded saying, "That sounds like something worth pursuing. How are you going to pay for it?" Dad's response was not a surprise to me. He wanted to hear our strategy. If the idea was worth pursuing, he was interested in the unfolding development process, which included the meticulous details that would lead to viability.

We have to make it a priority to answer the questions, "How are you going to pay for it?" and "What is your strategy?" In the work of creating positive social change, we have to make it a priority to address the vital details of operation and sustainability. There are four pillars of social sustainability named by the United Nations, through the Circles of Sustainability approach. These four pillars are human, social, economic, and environmental. How do we see sustainability through these lenses? To do so, it will often require a shift. The shift couldn't be more important than it is today, as we face many challenges and vital issues in America — the COVID-19 pandemic, systemic racism, white fragility, political unrest, climate change, unemployment, the availability and affordability of healthcare, equitable access to education, hunger and homelessness, etc.

Creating positive social change in our world today demands that we believe we can do it. The need to shift from a posture of scarcity to a position of abundance — or seeing the glass half full rather than half empty — is a critical orientation from which to build. A spirit of collaboration, humility, solid leadership, and strategic planning are essential to reaching your goals. Often organizational leaders elevate power and position over developing new processes that upset existing structures and move the organization toward sustainability. Therefore, a culture of innovation, entrepreneurship, and integrity are essential for creating positive social change.

A central attribute typically sought in potential innovative leaders is that of an "entrepreneurial spirit." Creating positive social change certainly demands an entrepreneurial spirit, which is evidenced through a person's natural proclivity for innovation. Innovators have to be creative risk-takers. Yet even with the desired and necessary predisposition, this attribute pushes against the boundaries of many leaders — both personal and organizational. The resulting anxiety can cause a number of destructive actions — avoiding risk completely, self-sabotage, shrinking from leadership, blaming others, avoidance, procrastination, and more.

The word entrepreneur, which is of French origin and means "one who undertakes," has traditionally been defined as "bearer of risk." The challenge is that many leaders do not have the business experience from which to lean into this valued attribute. Because of this, it is essential to discern how to engage one's entrepreneurial spirit from a sociological position, while embracing failure as a key building block and pivot forward.

So, how do we leverage all the assets we have available in a way that cultivates change in the circumstances of people's lives? How do we pivot from individual gain to an equitable community — where my life is not full until your life is full?[1] These are important process questions, which bring us to a larger one: What is the basis that represents **social entrepreneurship**?

In many ways it starts with liberation. Liberation must be a central motivator in the effort to change circumstances — the many necessary pivots from old, tired, and destructive strategies toward new, equitable, abundant ways of celebrating life together. Solutions are developed, funded, implemented, measured, and improved for the greater good of humanity.

> *Social Entrepreneurship is (1) Recognizing and resourcefully pursuing opportunities to create social value; (2) Crafting innovative approaches to addressing critical social needs. See: https://centers.fuqua.duke.edu/case/about/what-is-social-entrepreneurship/*

In the concept of **social entrepreneurship**, we must not leverage consumer posture for our own advantage. While we may not always be selling a product, it can be perceived that way. Any interaction with our target audience will likely be seen through a marketing lens. Therefore, the audience will judge our proposition in varying ways. They might quietly ask, "What's in it for me?" This is how "bait and switch" has been used to do harm.

---

[1] This idea of "my life is not full until your life is full," is based on the Lilla Watson quote, "If you have come here to help me, you are wasting your time. But if you have come because your liberation is bound up with mine, then let us work together."

What I am getting at here is **motive**. Will you leverage consumer posture for personal gain and influence? Or, will you subvert it for equitable community for positive social change? We have to change how we exist and co-create in the world, in order to rebuild trust and the resulting relationships necessary to change the world. This kind of change involves **integrity** — both individual and organizational. We must steward certain practices almost to perfection in order to help ensure sustainability and growth.

Throughout our work in community and economic development and engagement in the Northwest, we have engaged the practices of: 1) **diversity**, **equity**, and **inclusion**; 2) **innovation and entrepreneurship**, and 3) **social impact and growth**. It is through these practices you can engage, check, and evaluate movement. Each informs the next, circling back to the start to begin again. These practices can be summarized in the following list:

In the practice of **DIVERSITY, EQUITY,** and **INCLUSION**

- Humanity deserves better, which is why diversity, equity, inclusion, and belonging (DEI) are vital in our world. We often embrace the idea of DEI, but fail to fully practice it in our schools, workplaces, social circles, and politics. When we fully embody DEI, then everyone is represented and has agency in the work of creating positive social change.
- If we are culturally self-aware, then we engage difference well.
- If we are culturally competent, then we confront power and privilege and all "isms."

In the practice of **INNOVATION** and **ENTREPRENEURSHIP**

- Managing change requires that innovation become a natural rhythm in our organizational culture. This demands a creative space for the entrepreneurial spirit to flourish, while at the same time establishing appropriate protocol at every level to both manage and reinforce the movement. When we are able to establish an organizational culture that embodies innovation and entrepreneurship, then we are on the road to managing and measuring impact.

- If the organization is flexible enough, then we will see new expressions — new opportunities, new people, new leadership.

- If social innovation and entrepreneurship become an embodied rhythm, then we are able to embrace opportunities and mitigate risk.

In the practice of **SOCIAL IMPACT** and **GROWTH**

- Cultivating positive social change involves the development of contextual programs — those that emerge out of the community and that create measurable impact, including policy change. Feedback loops are essential, allowing us to pivot, improve, and scale the work appropriately. When we participate in active social impact and growth, then we create sustainable engagement that lasts.

- If a diversity of leaders are identified and developed, then leadership is expanded and new ways of leading emerge.

- If assets (economic, knowledge, network, innovation, human, and physical, etc.) are leveraged appropriately, then sustainability and growth are achieved at scale.

In order to engage the practices through the lens of positive social change, there are four primary areas we believe are important. These areas include:

- Diversity, equity, and inclusion
- Strategies that engage community organizing
- Asset-based community development (ABCD)
- Capacity building and sustainable growth

In order to shift from a aspirational tendency to innovation, we must emphasize a contextualized approach by integrating these four areas of resourcing. This means that it's not one area that is emphasized in positive social change. Instead, it's a measure of all four, shaped by context and deep listening. In order to rewire our tendency to match a program with a problem, our hope is to help you develop a variety of skills and strategies that are used together in contextual problem-solving. Think of it like ingredients for different recipes or a number of many available tools in your toolbox.

This will help you answer a number of questions, such as the following:

- How are you going to pay for "it"?
- How does the work of intercultural competency fit in with shaping a vision?
- Why is asset-based community development important to the work of strategic planning and growth?
- How do you engage in deep listening that can allow for the de-centering of white voices?
- How is social policy influenced?

These and many other questions come into view in the work of sustaining community engagement that makes a difference — that creates positive social change in the world, one neighborhood at a time.

We will begin with an overview of the model, and then address why you should consider using the process and how to use it, followed by the importance of team. Then we will get into each of the process blocks defined, which will include prompting questions that should result in action steps. Finally, we will walk through a summary and practical steps that give shape to a strategic plan for your organization and/or social enterprise.

SECTION 1:
The Strategic Planning Process

This section offers an overview of The Strategic Planning Process, why it should be considered, how to use it, and the importance of team.

CHAPTER 1
Overview: The Strategic Planning Process

In 2016, as a part of our consulting work in the Greater Northwest Area, I introduced the New Place Startup Process — strategic planning canvas — as a tool to offer a new approach to the planning and implementation process in creating positive social change. The framing is much like starting a new business. This canvas/process was based on the 2004 research of Alexander Osterwalder. What he produced was a unique way to map out a business model, providing space for creativity on a blank canvas — a way of engaging the organizational process. For entrepreneurs in the startup world, it was delivered as the **"business**

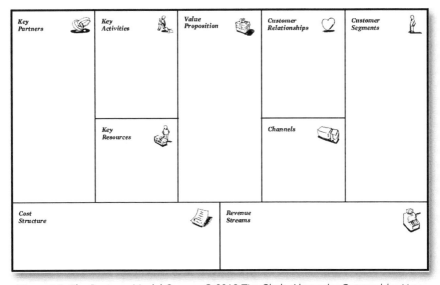

Figure 1.1. The Business Model Canvas. © 2012 Tim Clark, Alexander Osterwalder, Yves Pigneur. All rights reserved.

*The **Business model Canvas,** developed by Alexander Osterwalder, can be reviewed in more detail at the following link: https:// www.strategyzer.com/ canvas/business-model-canvas*

model canvas." This canvas presented nine separate areas, each labeled according to an essential component of most business models (see Figure 1.1).

These blank sections included at the center a "value proposition" (the product or service), flanked on the right by "customer segments" (the people or groups the business aims to reach and serve), "customer relationships" (the types of relationships the company establishes with customer groups), and "channels" (how the company communicates with and reaches the customer groups).

Flanked on the left side of the value proposition you find "key partners" (network of strategic partners), "key activities" (the most important things that must be done to make things work), and "key resources" (physical, intellectual, human, and financial resources). Below these six were two final sections: "cost structure" (costs incurred to operate) on the left, and "revenue streams" (cash generated from customer groups) on the right.

The canvas makes a way for entrepreneurs to list out components and strategies within each section (using Post-it notes or written notes on a white board), allowing for the ideas to be rearranged, edited, and seen together in the larger picture of the business model. Initially, this provided a visual way to collect and give shape to the building blocks that can inform a more robust business plan. For the entrepreneurial innovator, this can provide an exercise through which to see the larger organizational picture of how the new project cultivates, supports, measures, and accomplishes its mission.

In order to facilitate this creative process, I took Osterwalder's business model canvas and morphed it into what I called the **"Strategic Planning Process"** — a strategic planning canvas. (Note: Osterwalder's model has also been adapted by Ash Mauya into the "Lean Canvas," for a varied approach to new business startup.) I have appropriately changed some of the section titles to reflect the nonprofit business orientation I feel best represents an existing or emerging social enterprise. This version of the canvas/process makes way for a practical approach to social entrepreneurship.

The categories allow space to name and develop the essential components of an innovative business model. They can then be translated into a working strategic plan, shaped by a particular context. It also more clearly shows how a social enterprise might fit. Within the emerging business model, the innovator can see how the most effective tools for a particular context will be integrated toward action steps.

Throughout the book we will refer to both the **business model** and the strategic plan. The **social enterprise business model** (and in some instances your business plan) is developed during business startup or to evaluate your operations processes. Separately, the strategic plan provides focus, direction, and action steps in order to move your organization from where it is currently to where you want it to go in the future. Both are vital pieces at different stages, during the launch, growth, and impact of your organization.

How we collaborate, identify, and grow new leaders, and build new innovative systems, is critical. The approach encourages leaders to take

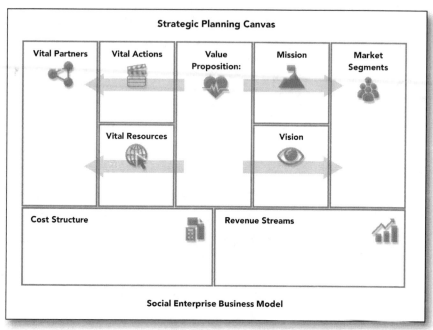

Figure 1.2. The Strategic Planning Canvas

a 30,000-foot view, while also narrowing down and identifying the practical steps that have to take place in each vital area of operation. Seeing the organization in this way should expose the right kind of questions to ask. It can drive how priorities are set, relationships are cultivated, leaders are identified, the market segments is engaged, and metrics are determined. The preceding illustration represents my version of the Strategic Planning Process for innovators, leaders, and social entrepreneurs. (see Figure 1.2).

This process contains nine areas that more closely represent the work of creating positive social change in the world. Each space will be explained in more detail in Section 2; however, here they are in summary:

1. **Value Proposition** — represents the product or proposed change. And though you may not be selling a "product," again, any strategic engagement within wider consumer culture is often interpreted through a marketing lens. Regardless, value proposition rests at the center of the work. (*Note: The faded arrows moving from the value proposition outward indicate that it permeates every part of the model.*)

> *The **Strategic Planning Process** is a morphed version of Osterwalder's business model canvas that we adapted to more closely reflect the components and considerations of nonprofit organizational development, specific to positive social change. The process will also reference the "**social enterprise business model**," which is specific to alternative revenue streams.*

2. **Market Segments** — represent the different people groups, communities, and organizations which make up the target audience you are trying to engage — the people or communities with which the social enterprise or initiative aims to collaborate and co-create.

3. **Vision** — how the new project communicates with, resonates, and reaches its audience to deliver a compelling value proposition. This is your elevator speech — how you describe *what can be*.

4. **Mission** — how the organization relates to its market segments in the process of community engagement and collaboration of positive change; *what we are compelled to do*. This is the rally cry for the change you are helping create in the world — your purpose (the who, what, and why).

5. **Vital Actions** — the most important tasks the new project must do to make its business model work. This will always represent a growing list that changes every season.

6. **Vital Resources** — the most important assets identified that will make the business model work. These include: economic, knowledge, network, innovation, as well as physical assets.

7. **Vital Partners** — the network of partners who have a natural connection or affinity to your new project, which helps make the business model work.

8. **Cost Structures** — represents all costs incurred to operate the new project and a 3-year budget to sustain the business model.

9. **Revenue Streams** — the revenue generated in the process of developing, reaching, and collaborating with your market segments/ target audience.

Each of these areas will be examined throughout this resource in the pattern order for developing a new initiative or social enterprise, which always begins by way of engaging your target audience. This pattern is highlighted in detail through the implementation parts of this resource. In Section 2, we will examine each of these nine areas/building blocks and the resulting actions that are a part of the social enterprise business model as a whole. The explanations will help show how the integration of tools and strategies support the larger, emerging social enterprise business model. In Section 3, we will bring everything together and help you produce a flexible and robust strategic plan.

CHAPTER 2
Why Consider this Process?

First and foremost, you do not have to use this process. But, it is essential to develop a detailed strategic plan that embodies flexibility and ultimately brings life, sustainability, and growth to your organization. If you are receiving funding (or going after funding) this kind of plan is critical to securing a sustainable and scalable future. However, it has to enable a cyclical process of research, experimentation, evaluation, learning, pivoting, and repeating — a positive feedback loop (discussed later in chapter 15).

It is clear that entrepreneurial gifts are important to leading new initiatives. However, too often organizational pushback squelches our best intentions to embrace new ways of operating in the world. Consequently, as innovative leaders, we tend to yield to expected patterns based on either tradition or security. Many new and young social entrepreneur leaders I have encountered over the years approached this work with two things in mind: money and staff. While both may be important at different times during the evolution of new initiatives, they are most certainly the least important initially. Most new business opportunities don't fail because of a lack of funding or staffing. They fail because of the lack of research, strategy, and planning.

My colleague Leroy Barber says that "innovation happens at the intersection of difference." This means that differences provide an opportunity — an innovative approach for a well-developed, adaptable plan. This kind of approach does not have to be weighted on the front end with high staffing costs and significant funding. Instead, it makes a way for a more lean approach that allows for learnings, and pivots in strategy, refinement, and scalability.

I have encouraged leaders to read Eric Ries' book, which was published in 2011 and titled, _The Lean Startup: How Today's Entrepreneurs Use Continuous Innovation to Create Radically Successful Businesses_. In his book, Ries argues that there are five principles that make up the lean startup approach. They include:

1. **Entrepreneurs are everywhere** — Ries believes entrepreneurs are represented by the human desire to create new products and services where significant risk exists and growth demands innovation.

2. **Entrepreneurship is management** — Ries also believes that startups are institutions, but they require new and innovative ways of management, which are geared to support extreme risk and uncertainty. Innovation fosters growth, which means it is critical to manage innovative ideas within a new institutional structure — one that does not institutionalize process.

3. **Validated learning** — Ries also argues that startup companies are not just about new products or making tons of money. They are about spaces for learning how to build sustainable models in an ever-changing consumer culture. It's about testing assumptions, experimentation, and making informed adjustments.

4. **Build-measure-learn** — Ries believes that startups are also about process. Specifically, it's about turning ideas into a value proposition, learning from consumer response, and making the necessary pivots in strategy. He names the importance of this feedback loop.

5. **Innovation accounting** — Ries also names what he calls the "boring stuff" of entrepreneurs; how progress is measured and the work is prioritized. While attention to these details is paramount, it demands flexible, new systems that support and reframe accountability.

In the work of community and economic development and positive social change, I have experienced leaders who have developed compelling visions in their effort to start a movement. Unfortunately, they often stop there, hoping that in casting a vision (and leaning on woo!), everyone will relate and everything will magically come together. This grave error reveals a number of problems. It fails to answer the most pressing unknowns — the most important, innovative tasks that must be tended for optimal performance of your organization. The strategy must also embrace failure as an opportunity to shift and adjust.

A flexible strategic plan contains creative space for an idea to become reality. While there is freedom to take risks and jump in, there must also be a culture that can mitigate the tension between disruptive innovation and the necessity for order. When organizations can remain in the uncertain space between the two, new ways forward become apparent.

Tension is necessary. In fact, the phrase "chaordic tension," which was first coined by Dee Hock, the founder of Visa (and embraced by the corporate culture of companies such as Disney), is paramount for the success of startups. In organizations that constantly navigate changing markets, this phrase describes the very real tug of war that exists between the desire for order and the necessity of chaos. Liberating institutions embody this kind of organizational culture, representing an organic flexibility that is oriented toward sustainability. This is the successful union of innovation and the organization.

*For an example of the **2022 strategic plan** of **FareStart**, check out the QR code below. Located in Seattle, Washington, **FareStart** "has been helping people transform their lives through food for nearly 30 years — one person, one job and one community at a time."*

In the world of startup, there must be a willingness to be OK with the irregularity that makes the work unique — entrepreneurial startups live on the edge. But, through the course of development, these social ventures must carve a path toward thoroughness that both grows and sustains the organization, allowing for new processes, systems, and ordered pathways. It is absolutely important to establish this kind of culture.

Don't misunderstand me; disruptive innovation absolutely needs space. Products and services evolve through a process of optimization, where chaordic tension encourages fine-tuning and pivots in strategy without compromising the overarching vision. The same must be true for a collaborative approach to starting new projects and initiatives. The implicit (and often unrecognized) desire for larger organizations to institutionalize almost everything must pivot toward innovation as a standard-bearer.

You must approach this work in the same vein as starting a new business, with solid research, strategic planning, and the necessity of sustainability. It will force you to operate in the important role of social innovator/entrepreneur. It also positions you to see your granting agency or funding sources in the same way entrepreneurs see venture capital firms.

For example, in the world of for-profit startup, the venture capital relationship is very straightforward. The union is represented in two partners: general and limited. While general partners do all the work, limited partners provide the funding. And typically, that is the end of the involvement of limited partne rs, outside of an expectation of a good return on investment (ROI). While our lane focuses on social enterprise and positive social change, noting the similarities with for-profit startup relationships can be helpful.

The bottomline is that if you have a dream, you have to figure out how you are going to pay for it into perpetuity. This will require multiple revenue streams, which will include many (if not all) of the following: startup funds, grants, personal network, donations, crowd funding, subscriptions, partnerships, social enterprise, and even endowments. Your strategic plan is incredibly important and will require constant attention. It provides the fuel that keeps the engine of your initiative or social enterprise operating at peak performance and accomplishing the stated mission.

Why utilize this process? Because the purpose for the Strategic Planning Process is to help you identify and integrate the kind of culture and organizational structure necessary for starting and sustaining new initiatives, projects, or social enterprises. For those who have not leaned into their own entrepreneurial spirit — or those who have not been in a space where this attribute has been encouraged — the process can simplify a compartmentalized approach that makes integrating tasks and strategy straightforward.

CHAPTER 3
How to Utilize the Strategic Planning Process

We will explain how to engage each building block separately in Section 2. That explanation will not only integrate the identified resourcing mentioned in the introduction — diversity, equity, and inclusion; community organizing; asset-based community development; and social impact and growth — but also provide starter questions and instructions. This will generate an action list for each building block of the process. However, before we jump into that work, we should understand how to use the process as a guide.

First, print out a large copy of the process canvas, or plot it on a poster board or dry-erase white board. Begin to consider each building block and how they relate. You should see the right side of the process as the **delivery** vehicle (**market segments, vision, mission**) for your project, and the left side of the process as the supporting or **operational** side (**vital actions, vital resources, vital partners**). Each of the blocks you engage should begin with a basic pattern, where the first informs the next, and so forth.

The following illustration (Figure 1.3) shows the beginning of this brainstorming, categorizing process. When you exhaust each list under each of the nine building blocks, your canvas should be well populated with ideas/considerations.

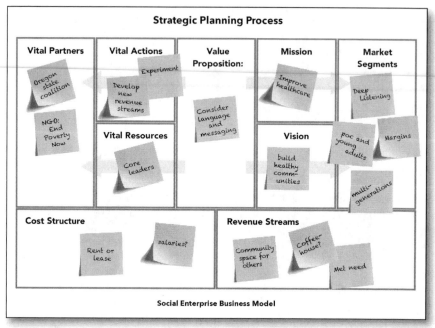

Figure 1.3

As you consider your emerging social enterprise business model, you will have a better sense of many patterns among the building blocks and how they give shape to your strategies and priorities. For instance, the activity of deep listening, within your market segments/target audience, will give shape to how you cultivate and communicate a vision. How you collect and cast vision can also help you understand various components of the mission, consequently helping you identify the vital actions that need to take place. Identifying the vital actions will help you determine what resources are needed (and those you have), what partners are necessary, and so forth.

As you begin to record all of these tasks and potential or existing partners, you will be able to identify your cost structure and how it places demand on your revenue streams. The illustration below (Figure 1.4) shows the previous description as a pattern on the planning process. Each pattern may be different, based on a number of factors, such as your market segments, the data you collect, the assumptions you test, the actions determined, the revenue streams needed, etc.

The value proposition will always influence and shape both the operations (vital actions, resources, partners, and cost structure) and delivery (mission, vision, market segments, and revenue streams) of the business model (hence the arrows moving outward from the center). Think of the process as a tool that helps you compartmentalize your strategic thinking. Hold it loosely and creatively. The exercise will help you see the mission from a crisp vantage and through a new lens. The process begins with deep listening, engaging the very people you hope

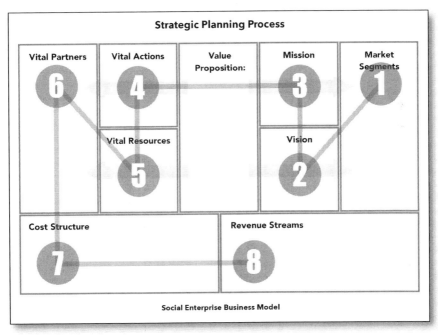

Figure 1.4

to reach and with whom to collaborate. Everything is built on these discoveries.

What are the next steps?

Once you have spent time considering each of the nine building blocks of the startup process and see how they relate to and inform one another, you will have much of the information needed to begin developing (or enhancing) a robust strategic plan. You can also discover what you are missing, your areas of weakness, the underused assets, collective big dreams, the real obstacles, and a much clearer picture of your market segments/target audience. All of this information is then used to set your priorities for next steps.

Utilizing the strategic planning process will help you construct the kind of flexible strategic plan necessary to accomplish effective engagement in your context. Before you dive into strategic plan development, which will be framed in Section 3, let us first move toward the importance of a solid team.

CHAPTER 4
The Importance of a Team

You cannot do this work alone, successfully. You can initiate it, but to think you can take on this work, scale it, and create something sustainable and meaningful on your own is a fool's errand. While the necessity of a team should go without saying, I want to take this opportunity to remind you that it's not just about forming a team; it's also about the cultural ethos you create. A spirit of collaboration is critical.

Things to keep in mind when building your team:

You definitely need a team you trust, and with whom you collaborate, cast your vision, hold one another accountable, and refine how you articulate the value proposition. Here are some things to consider:

1. **Understand what you are after** — Knowing your vision and mission is the centerpiece to building a solid team. If you do not know what your end-game is — your mission — you will not be able to engage and partner with committed team members. Your team members must buy-in to the vision and mission and be willing to carry that torch with you.

2. **Culture and intercultural competency** — Your team needs to reflect the people groups you are trying to engage and your communication and decision-making processes must reflect equity and agency for those groups. Not only is it important to understand culture from multiple perspectives — organizational culture, cultural

Photo credit: You X Ventures, Unsplash.com

self-awareness, racial and ethnic identities, among others — but also it is vital to the formation of your team. Intercultural competency should be foundational to the work we do and, therefore, must rest at the center of forming a solid team. Shifting from individualism to the collective and common good of all has to be inseparable from considerations around diversity, equity, and inclusion.

3. **Deconstructing a colonial mindset** — Colonization is embedded within American culture. Therefore, if it is not considered and addressed in the formation of your team, conformity and assimilation will impede innovation. Moreover, it will limit your team's ability to bring their full self to the work. If not addressed, dominance and exploitation become central. In contrast, a decolonized team represents, honesty, integrity, transparency in communication, and respect.

4. **Gifts and experience** — You and I are incapable of doing everything, which also means there are some areas in our skill sets that are either deficient or nonexistent. Surround yourself with qualified people who are gifted in ways you are not. Experience matters.

5. **Refine your vision** — Culture is always emerging — the world and our collective circumstances are shifting. As you navigate the ever-changing landscape, and while also refining your vision, make sure you stay focused on the vision. And make sure this translates to the areas of focus for each of your team members.

6. **Celebrate the opportunities that difference brings** — It is vital to become hyperaware that there are new ways of doing, thinking, and being in the world. A diverse team that is fully engaged brings about diverse opportunities and innovative strategy. This is especially important around influencing social policy.

7. **A spirit of collaboration** — While good team members are driven, egos must be checked at the door. A spirit of collaboration is paramount for an effective team. Strong teams fail together and succeed together. It's not about you.

Discussion and Planning Questions Related to Building Your Team:

1. What is your plan for identifying potential leaders?

2. How are you building diversity, equity, and inclusion into your leadership?

    a.   Does your board reflect the wider community members with which you are collaborating?

3. What is your plan for addressing issues of power and privilege and for engaging Black, Indigenous, and people of color (BIPOC) voices or other non-dominant cultures on your team?

4. How will you cultivate safe and courageous space for people to join into the movement?

5. Describe what a spirit of collaboration might look like in your new project/initiative/social enterprise.

SECTION 2:
Process Blocks Defined and Engaged

This section offers an overview of each process block, along with questions/considerations, categories of connections, and helpful discussion and planning questions for each block. These can then be integrated into the whole of the process.

CHAPTER 5
Value Proposition

Within the context of developing a strategic plan for positive social change, the value proposition should represent the value your organization offers your community and world. Keep in mind, that in the Strategic Planning Process, the first step is to engage your market segments. However, the value proposition, is central and informs the entire process of strategic planning (see Fig. 1.4 on page 31). The value proposition should embody the contextual problem you are compelled to solve. It's the why — the reason the community turns to your organization to fulfill the need or gap in services.

What value do you offer? What needs are being met? Your **value proposition** represents a promise of value that your organization will provide. It may be a product/service or a grouping of products or services that fall into a particular category. For example, if your value proposition falls under the category of "wellness," you might offer the products/services connected to emotional/mental, occupational, physical, environmental, financial, or spiritual well-being. Your value proposition might be the result of innovation, or there could be similarities to other offers with added features or improved options.

At the very core of our humanness often rests a desire to embrace all that life is supposed to offer, even when we do not fully know what that might look like (this will be different for everyone). It is even more important to recognize that in creating social change, liberation is at the center — again; my life is not full until your life is full. Therefore, your

Photo credit: Austin Schmid, unsplash.com.

value proposition must bend toward the challenges and needs you have identified within your mission statement.

When it comes to culture and context, the language you use to represent the value proposition is driven by what you know and learn from your wider community. By comparison, in the private sector no company would blindly offer a product at market without interacting and collaborating with their many people groups. Again, in consumer culture, where our engagement is evaluated through a marketing lens, we must intimately know our community and translate the value proposition in every area it permeates. There are many considerations to be addressed, many of which can be framed through the following questions:

- What have you learned about your market segments (characteristics) that would shape the language you use to express value?

- What value does your organization offer to improve the quality of life for individuals?
- How do the people groups gather their information, communicate with, and engage one another?

Characterization of the **value proposition** is incredibly important, representing the service or product/program that delivers the organization's vision/mission. They are the distinguishing features that point to something larger and inform your communication plan.

Formation of the **value proposition** can be described through the following two perspectives and how those in your market segments may interpret the value:

Community perspective:

1. Safe space

   - Is this a safe space where one can bring her/his/their full self/selves?

2. Justice, equity, and racial reconciliation

   - How does social justice both shape and represent the value proposition?

   - Do marginalized voices have full access and agency?

3. Disruptive innovation and creativity

   - Are new ways forward given room to emerge and actively disrupt the status quo?

- How do learnings inform new strategies?

- What does success look like through the lens of your value proposition?

4. Contextualization and translation

- In what ways are you allowing community context to dictate how the value proposition is communicated and positioned?

- Do you know how your value proposition is perceived across your market segments/people groups/communities?

Consumer perspective:

1. Branding, positioning, and design

- How is the value proposition experienced through the aesthetics of images, words, and spaces?

- Does shared brand equity exist through a vital partner?

2. Excellence and brand awareness

- In an American consumer culture, people are conditioned to look for quality and the best value. How will this inform or subvert the interpretation of the value proposition?

42

- How is quality assurance achieved?

3. Communication strategies

   - Knowing how your audience and your community gets access to information, communicates with others, and shares experiences, is essential. How will this shape your communication strategies?

   - How will your target audience inform those strategies?

4. Audience perception (does the message match the action?)

   - Based on a prevalent American consumer culture, how will your understanding of a consumer perspective help you subvert skepticism and embrace integrity?

   - Another way to think about this is through the lens of "hypocrisy." Do your actions reflect your words?

You will have a higher chance of engaging your target communities through a clear value proposition — you will be communicating directly to them and providing a solution to their identified needs. Not only is your value proposition a great way to increase brand awareness, but it is the single most important piece to your overall marketing and communication strategies.

*Your **value proposition** is a key driver to meeting a specific need (or needs) in your community or region. To learn more, check out how **Bread of Life, Inc.**, led by Pastors Rudy and Juanita Rasmus in Houston, Texas, is meeting a basic community need, and so much more.*

Discussion and Planning Questions Related to the Value Proposition:

Now it's time to take a step forward.

1. Considering how we have examined the Value Proposition, how would it be shaped for your own context?

2. Your strategy must be informed by listening to your target audience. Good one-to-one conversations are critical (see the next chapter, which includes one-to-one sessions).

3. What is the promise of value you plan to deliver to your target audiences?

CHAPTER 6
Market Segments

Do you really know your community? Are you actively building new relationships? Are you learning new things about the world through contact with new people? Do you understand the cultural dynamics at play — the many cultures and subcultures represented, which shape people, traditions, and cultural norms? How many people groups does your organization engage? And for what purposes?

When we integrate a community organizing approach to our work, we not only strive to change how we see our communities, but we also change the way in which we engage and learn. Community organizing moves us from a position of isolation and self-interest to a collaborative approach that embraces the whole.

In his book *Community: The Structure of Belonging*, Peter Block sets up the provocation. He writes:

> The essential challenge is to transform the isolation and self-interest within our communities into connectedness and caring for the whole. The key is to identify how this transformation occurs. We begin by shifting our attention from the problems of community to the possibilities of community. We also need to acknowledge that our wisdom about individual transformation is not enough when it comes to community transformation. The purpose here is to bring together our knowledge about the nature of collective transformation. A key insight in this pursuit is to accept the importance of social capital to the life of

45

the community. This begins the effort to create a future distinct from the past.[2]

Your **market segments** represents the different people groups, neighborhoods, communities, and organizations which make up the particular audience with which you hope to serve, partner, and co-create. Every community reflects a unique context where people groups gather for social, economic, professional, and personal reasons.

Each market segment is nuanced by our human interaction, while our assumptions are drawn from the many biases and lenses through which we view the world. Though there may be general reasons people are found together in certain areas (e.g., political preference, ethnicity), there also may be varying degrees that are not clearly perceived.

In order to better understand common ground, behaviors, priorities, and other attributes, we must first understand the many cultures and subcultures that make up our communities. Reviewing basic demographics will shape perception, requiring you to unpack assumptions. When we put people in compartments, we can make the mistake of sweeping assumptions (e.g., millennials are self-absorbed and entitled, Gen-Xers are the slacker generation, or Baby Boomers are the real problem). Surface assumptions and implicit bias can sabotage your strategies. This is why we have to uncover our assumptions and engage our target audience through deep listening. Relationships are key.

While broader information and characteristics can be discovered through comprehensive demographic studies, one-to-one listening is a practice of community organizing that exposes more than data. In this

---

[2] Peter Block, *Community: The Structure of Belonging,* (Oakland: Berrett-Koehler, 2018), 1.

work you will find the heartbeat of a community, originating from the passion and challenges of the people who live there. Demographic information can give you a snapshot, but it needs to be verified and made more robust through the practice of listening.

There are a number of considerations when approaching your market segments, including:

- Who lives in your community?
  - Are there people groups with which you do not relate? Why?
  - Where are BIPOC voices in your setting?
  - Does your new project reflect the diversity of your neighborhood? If not, why not?
- How culturally and ethnically diverse is you target audience?
- What are the things you do not know about your target audience?
- What is the greatest identified need?
- Have you identified who holds the power?
- How would you assess the risk the audience is willing to take together?
- What inspires your target audiences?
- What groups or organizations have successfully developed relationships with your particular audience?
  - How can you learn from and/or partner with these groups/organizations?

As you reflect on your target audiences, think about how the following categories intersect and help you categorize, prioritize, and understand people groups:

- Demographics
- Ethnic difference (multicultural)
- Those people outside your social circles
- Those people inside your social circles
- Ages and stages (multi-generational)
- Other sociological considerations
- Political positions

When you begin to identify the market you might serve there are a number of ways to categorize these segments (in addition to what I have listed above). This is particularly important when you begin to work through your business model and how market segments intersect and support the mission of your organization. Steve Zimmerman offers a more holistic view of the nonprofit market and how different segments relate to the organization. Zimmerman uses the image of a "market wheel" to describe the intersection points nonprofits must consider. He describes the five components[3] of the "market wheel" segments as follows:

- **Direct Beneficiaries** (those who use the organization's products or services)
- **Other Beneficiaries/Funders** (wider groups who benefit from the organization's efforts, values, ideals, etc.)

---

[3] Steve Zimmerman, "Community Influences: Understanding Nonprofit Markets," Nonprofit Quarterly, https://nonprofitquarterly.org/community-influences-understanding-nonprofit-markets/ (accessed December 29, 2020).

- **Other Organizations** (both for-profit and nonprofit partners who might share the target audiences)
- **Input/Labor Market** (representing the human capital of staff, volunteers, board members, etc.)
- **Political/Social Environment** (the environment that influences the organization's ability to achieve its mission)

The components Zimmerman highlights will certainly shape your business model. He reminds us that the single most important driving component influencing strategies the most is that of your direct beneficiaries. The people who benefit from the products/services your organization can provide the best information you will collect. This allows you and your leaders to shape strategy and measure impact more effectively. Again, deep listening is key. It's why community organizing strategies can be valuable to understanding your market segments.

Gathering people together, empowering their gifts, and mobilizing them at the grassroots level to act together are the basic tenants of community organizing. The initial interaction and learning within our market segments actually begins by developing relationships that matter. Our interaction with identified target audiences is the bedrock for building a business model that actually makes a difference and changes circumstances in our communities. What we learn, the relationships we establish, and the actions that develop, point toward *what can be* — a vision.

However, when it comes to deep listening, there is an important consideration: One-to-one interaction cannot be motivated from the position of numbers. In other words, your one-to-ones must come about from a position of sincere curiosity — an authentic desire to establish a

*Your **market segments** represent people who, given voice and agency, will uncover need and show the way toward necessary change. Check out the **Poor People's Campaign: A National Call for Moral Revival.***

relationship with the person, one of collaboration. It's not based on trying to convince one out of 10 people to join your movement.

Remember, this is not about selling the person anything. It's about listening, in order to learn about hopes, dreams, passion, gifts, needs, contributions, etc. Meaningful conversation means that you listen more than you talk. Community organizing tools are for the purpose of building community. They are for engaging, learning, and empowering people to act. And, they can help give shape to an emerging vision that is compelling — one that actually starts a movement.

Within our Northwest context, there are two familiar community organizing groups:

- **IAF Northwest** — a regional network of the larger Industrial Areas Foundation (IAF), a community organizing alliance that works "to build individual civic leadership, strengthen its member organizations, and to serve as a vehicle for these members to act in the public arena with sufficient power for the common good." For more information, visit: iafnw.org.

- **Faith In Action** — a federation network that focuses on improving lives through "faith-based community organizations working to create innovative solutions to problems facing urban, suburban and rural communities." For more information, visit: faithinaction.org.

Examples of One-to-One Listening Sessions

Not to sound repetitive, but one-to-one conversations are not used to manipulate others nor are they used to convince someone of something. They are opportunities for deep listening and a tool for building authentic relationships. These conversations, allow you to test and set aside your assumptions. To quote Ted Lasso, misattributing Walt Whitman, "Be curious, not judgmental."[4] Not only can you gain insight as to what motivates other people, but also you will identify existing and future leaders in your neighborhood/community.

1. **One-to-ones (again) are not about selling anything** — You are not pitching your vision or even naming a task for someone to engage. You should focus on the person and their story.

2. **One-to-ones (again) are about listening** — Your objective is to try to see and understand the world from the other person's perspective. You should do more listening than talking. Model a rule of 75% listening and 25% talking.

3. **One-to-ones are short** — Your initial meet-up should not be a major commitment for the other person. Name the length of time you would like to meet when you make the invite (30 to 45 minutes).

4. **One-to-ones are not for therapy** — Your conversation partner is not your therapist, nor are you your conversation partner's therapist.

---

[4] "The Diamond Dogs," *Ted Lasso*, created by Jason Sudeikis, Bill Lawrence, Brendan Hunt, and Joe Kelly, Season 1, Episode 8, Warner Bros. Television Distribution, 2020.

Photo credit: Cristina Morillo, pexels.com

5. **One-to-ones help uncover tension** — By listening and beginning to see the world from the other person's perspective, you will be able to discover what people are concerned about in their neighborhoods.

6. **One-to-ones are not recruiting sessions** — Your deep listening sessions are not a time for recruitment. Resist the urge to invite the person onto your team. Listen for a more robust story. Be patient.

7. **One-to-ones (again) help identify leaders** — By listening to the other person's story, you can discover what they are involved in and what leadership roles they have held in their work.

8. **One-to-ones are not about fixing things** — These sessions are not about helping an individual solve a problem. Resist problem-solving and focus on hearing the other person.

9. **One-to-ones are about being fully present** — Deep listening is an engaging activity. In addition to listening well, make sure you pay attention to your body language and make eye contact, when culturally appropriate to do so. Honor the other person's engagement.

One-to-One Listening is an organizing conversation that is ultimately about getting to a place of action — and next steps — from a foundation of deep listening, so that you are able to understand where someone else is coming from and what common goals and values you might share. It's about learning and being curious.

Discussion and planning questions for the Market Segments that can shape the value proposition:

1. Discuss the learnings of the target audience and how they shape they way you communicate about the value proposition.

2. What values are identified and how will those values be embodied?

3. What is your plan for meeting new people?

4. What needs were you able to identify and how will you allow the voices who identified or affirmed these needs collaborate with you in framing the value proposition?

   a. What are the hopes, dreams, and possibilities of those you listen to and how do they align with the hopes and dreams to which you are compelled?

5. How are the characteristics of the identified values present in your engagement, without having to explicitly point them out?

6. How sensitive are you to the formation of this value through the community, and consumer perspectives (lenses) in every outlet through which you engage the target audience and community?

CHAPTER 7
Vision

Vision = What can be. The **vision** represents how you've listened to your target audiences and delivered your value proposition. Deep listening to the people groups within identified market segments gives shape to a vision that inspires *what can be*. Having the ability to effectively articulate your **vision** is central to cultivating new relationships/partnerships and sparking a movement. When someone asks you what you are up to, what do you say? What is your elevator speech?

Vision statements are not visions. They are sentences that offer an abbreviated and concise expression of intentional direction — opportunities that matter. In the corporate world, more often than not, vision statements are less about making a difference and more about making money, wrapped in the cloak of making a difference. In the nonprofit sector, they illuminate the impact and emerging positive social change.

For-profit companies spend significant energy becoming crystal clear about how to connect and communicate with their particular market in ways that manipulate buying decisions and promote brand loyalty. Positioning a brand as a "lifestyle" is one way companies might align with the notion of "community impact." Market research shapes products and the strategies employed to distribute and sell those products.

In order to spark a movement of social change in your community, the vision must represent the hopes and dreams of people groups within your market segments. This means that intercultural competency remains as a foundation for the development of your own cultural self-awareness, how you understand place, and how you appreciated the vast range of perspectives that often exist in our communities. What are the hopes and dreams of your neighbors? Where do you find intersecting points within the market segments? How big is the collective dream? You want to hold a birthing vision carefully and with open hands.

In important ways, this has to become personal. Being curious about people in your community will help you discover what they may already be up to. Unless you are scaling a successful model, you should not take a cookie-cutter approach. Instead, you should discover what is emerging from the action and organizing in your community. This is how a grassroots movement takes shape. Where do you see others already at work making a difference in the community?

The vision statement — your elevator speech — should clearly articulate the hopes and dreams of your organization, inspiring others to join in the movement, while making room for new voices. Here are some considerations as you develop your vision statement:

1. **Clear:** Make sure the primary goal is apparent.

2. **Bold:** Your vision must be compelling and point toward change — "Get into good trouble, necessary trouble" (Rep. John Lewis).

3. **Future-oriented:** The vision is "what can be" — the difference to be actuated and celebrated.

Photo credit: Riccardo Annandale, <u>unsplash.com</u>

4. **Challenging:** Bold visions embrace innovation; they initiate action, in response to disruption.

5. **Inspiring:** Why should someone care? A strong vision statement lifts the hopes and dreams of others to action.

6. **Contextual:** The vision must be in response to the challenges and opportunities within a specific context.

Aspirational statements might feel good, but they must also reflect what is being lived out in community. A vision statement should provide others an entry point of engagement, while inspiring the difference that can be achieved together. It should embody the ultimate goal — e.g., *common good for the neighborhood.* What will you and your community partners dream together?

The following are some examples of vision statements from leading corporations and nonprofit organizations. Notice how they invoke a lifestyle, pushing the narrative away from products and services to a particular way of being in the world. This marketing strategy is how culture is shaped, both within an organization and within a specific market.

Nike — "Bring inspiration and innovation to every athlete* in the world. (*If you have a body, you are an athlete.")

Patagonia — "Build the best product, cause no unnecessary harm, use business to inspire and implement solutions to the environmental crisis."

American Heart Association — "To be a relentless force for a world of longer, healthier lives."

Apple — "We believe that we are on the face of the earth to make great products and that's not changing."

Microsoft — "Microsoft is a technology company whose mission is to empower every person and every organization on the planet to achieve more. We strive to create local opportunity, growth, and impact in every country around the world."

Habitat for Humanity — "A world where everyone has a decent place to live."

REI — "REI's core purpose is to inspire, educate, and outfit for a lifetime of outdoor adventure and stewardship. As a cooperative, everyone in the company and customers, producers, and suppliers, are invited in to the mission of REI and asked to play a part in creating the unique REI experience."

Goodwill — "Every person has the opportunity to achieve his/her fullest potential and participate in and contribute to all aspects of life."

Alaska Airlines — "To be one of the most respected U.S. airlines by our customers, employees, and shareholders."

Google — "To provide access to the world's information in one click."

Amazon — "Our vision is to be earth's most customer-centric company; to build a place where people can come to find and discover anything they might want to buy online."

NPR — "To produce, acquire, and distribute programming that meets the highest standards of public service in journalism and cultural expression; to represent our members in matters of their mutual interest, and to provide satellite interconnection for the entire public radio system."

Remember, your vision is your elevator speech. It represents **what can be**. It must come from deep listening to the people and places of your community — the target audiences/market segments. It's how we deliver our value proposition.

Discussion and Planning Questions for Shaping the Vision:

1. Where does difference convene in your context? How can your new project bring difference together?

2. What new things do you want to explore or pioneer?

3. Name the positive risks that need to happen for your project to be successful.

4. How do the answers to these questions help shape **what can be** in your context?

CHAPTER 8
Mission

Mission = What we are compelled to do.

The mission represents how your
organization, project, or initiative relates to
your identified people groups. Remember, if liberation is at the core of
our social justice action, then the idea that "my life is not full until your
life is full" must continue to be reflected in our words and our actions.
Culture shift begins with language and how we talk about the necessary
social change we hope for (the vision — *what can be*).

Your mission defines how you relate to your target audiences/market
segments. If the vision is *what can be*, then the mission is *what we are
compelled to do*. Most people want to do the right thing and align
themselves with others who feel the same. Having a clear mission both
orients your organization toward solving a specific problem (or set of
problems) and invites others into that work. If vision describes the
aspirational vantage of possibilities, the mission turns your organization's
assets and energy into a process of moving beyond a dream to the
practical actions that help us realize the dream.

The United States didn't live into the mission of going to the moon
without first naming that hope and dream well before all the problems
were solved — years ahead the historic date of July 20, 1969, when
astronauts first walked on the moon (mission accomplished). We must
strive diligently for our "actions" to align with our "words." That is how
we move the needle of change.

Photo credit: Mark Konig, *unsplash.com*

If the actions of the mission must embody the dreams of the vision, then how do you get there? Here are some thoughts:

1. **Hone your mission** — Your mission — your organization's purpose — represents why you do what you do. As you develop your mission statement, take into consideration what it is that makes your organization stand apart. What is compelling about the work? Just as consumers will often buy what advertisers tell them to buy, most employees will do what they think their leaders want. Name it.

2. **Know how your vision informs the mission** — Too often, organizations confuse mission and vision statements. While I have already framed this, it is helpful to remember that **vision** = *what can be*, and **mission** = *what we are compelled to do*. Understanding this link will help you shape how the vision informs the mission of your

organization. And, as a leader (or your leadership team) you must revisit this regularly to make sure there is both alignment and appropriate targeting.

3. **Include the values of your organization** — Just as your vision informs the mission, how you get things done must also embody certain cultural values. For example, if diversity, equity, and inclusion (DEI) represents a value of your organization, how does that show up in the mission? When you are able to articulate your values, you are setting certain expectations of behavior for your employees and team. This influences how you get the work done.

4. **Cultivate alignment with your team, processes, and protocol** — Once you have honed your mission, you need everyone in the organization moving in sync toward accomplishing it. Alignment must exist in every aspect of your organizational culture. If alignment does not exist, there will be mission creep, unmet goals, inefficiency, and poor stewardship. When everyone understands what they contribute, and how, productivity is the result.

5. **Keep the mission in front of you and your team** — Your mission must inform every aspect of your organization — the communications plan; listening inside and outside the company; informing how decisions are made and strategy is implemented; how success is measured; how employees and volunteers bring their full selves to the work, etc. Make sure you keep the mission front and center in every part of your organization.

Remember, the mission is *what we are compelled to do.* It represents the action and movement toward *what can be* — the vision — and it represents your organization's purpose. Based on the identified values of your organization, it orients your team, employees, and volunteers toward future growth and positive social change. And, it encourages everyone to think about how their actions align with that purpose.

The Emergence of Strategic Goals

Finally, the mission serves as the beginning point — the foundation — for the development of your strategic goals. Strategy is directly linked and shaped by the vision and mission of the organization. This is the birthplace for strategic planning and alignment. Naming your strategic goals is evidence that you and your leaders are mapping out what growth looks like — progress and success. It is important to begin to identify the goals that provide evidence of the mission in action. These also become the initial targets that shape the metrics you will use to measure success.

Examples of strategic goals could include the following:

- 30% increase in volunteer participation
- 100 one-to-one listening sessions completed and reported each month
- Conduct quarterly intercultural competency trainings for staff and volunteers
- 50% increase in donor retention rate
- 500 clients served in each reporting quarter of year one
- 25% increase in jobs gained through workforce development programs
- 25 community events held
- 40% increase in the number community advocates trained

- Develop 10 new contextual programs that help meet an identified need and expand the impact of our organization and its vital partners
- Ensure that the composition of our board reflects the people groups we work with and the skill sets needed to move the organization forward
- Establish a robust communication plan

Discussion Questions for the Mission:

1. How does your vision inform the mission?

2. What are the core cultural values of your organization?

3. What is your plan for learning and growing community across cultural difference?

4. What power and privilege do you (individually and corporately) represent in this context?

5. What issues disproportionally impact vulnerable communities and what movements will you engage to correct them?

6. Based on your work to hone the mission of your organization, begin to list your strategic goals that help move the organization toward achieving the mission.

Clarity in the mission and how you will accomplish it allows for important boundaries within your organization — how you share responsibility, delegate tasks, and exercise judgement. It's like the headlamp, pointing the way and navigating you toward measurable results. Mission clarity provides transparency that is important for your stakeholders.

CHAPTER 9
Vital Actions

Vital actions represent the most important things you must do to make the business model work, from within the overall strategic plan. Every new project/initiative/program has a number of to-dos that push the movement forward in order to cultivate success. But with vital actions, I'm not talking about your long to-do list. Instead, this section represents the most important actions that must happen in order to accomplish the organization's mission.

These actions are both a result of considering your value proposition, while also giving shape to how the vision is perceived and received by people groups. Vital actions generate costs on various levels — financial, human, time, etc. — contributing to a better understanding of energy spent in any given season of your project/programs. Different business models require different actions and energy.

For instance, if you were starting a bakery (even as a social enterprise), the vital actions might be baking, delivery, advertising/marketing, and building and optimizing your business platform. These actions are the most important to establishing your bakery and providing a process through which to evaluate and pivot strategy. While there is a myriad of to-dos in a new bakery, the vital actions are the most important activities that push the strategic planning process closer to a sustainable model. The same will be true for your organization. Your vital actions should reflect the operations side of your business model (vital actions, vital resources, and vital partners), as it relates to the delivery side (the

Photo credit: Álvaro Serrano, *unsplash.com*.

market segments, vision, and mission). There shouldn't be more than four or five vital actions for your project/program/initiative.

Of course, there are differences in models that account for basic differences in vital actions. For instance, a bakery produces items to sell — cakes, cookies, breads, etc. Selling these products accounts for the primary revenue stream. So, all necessary vital actions are the ones that help achieve this transaction (baking, delivery, advertising, and building and optimizing the business platform).

In starting a new project/program/initiative you can begin your focus primarily on four areas: **People**, **Communication Plan**, **Financial Sustainability**, and **Evaluation and Assessment**.

People:

As we have already discussed on the delivery side of the canvas/process, the market segments, vision, and mission all relate to how we engage, communicate, and co-create with specific people groups/audience. Here are a few things to consider under the people category:

1. **Cultural Self-awareness** — The work of diversity, equity, and inclusion is ongoing within your organization. Gaining awareness of your own cultural values, norms, communication style, and worldview allows you to appreciate the cultural formation and experiences of others. Cultural differences make for more effective teams, which engages more voices to influence strategies. *How will the work of diversity, equity, and inclusion continue to shape how your organization sees and engages others?*

2. **Meeting new people** — Positive social change centers on creating a movement through aligned relationships. This centers on engaging new people, networking relationships, and establishing new partners. *What is your plan for inviting new people to join in your movement?*

3. **Deep Listening** — Hearing the stories and experiences of others in your context allows you to test and suspend assumptions and learn from others. *How will you hear the needed voices that contribute to an inspiring vision and compelling mission?*

4. **Building Relationships** — It's one thing to meet someone new and hear his/her/their story. It is quite another to build authentic relationships with others who share in an unfolding vision and

grassroots movement. *What is your plan for collaborating with others?*

Communication Plan:

Naming a basic communication strategy is essential to your startup efforts. In a day and time when new information is accessed almost immediately, it is essential to continue to build a communication strategy. Here are a few things to consider to get you started:

1. **Elevator Speech** — Your vision in short form, the elevator speech should permeate how you talk about the work you see emerging in your context. *What are the creative ways you will utilize your elevator speech to build awareness and cast vision?*

2. **Talking Points** — While your elevator speech is your personal/team response of passion, talking points provide a way to coalesce messaging. Make sure you develop clear talking points that can be utilized by your board members, ED, team, staff, and volunteers.

3. **Personal Platform** — In an era where social capital and influence has become a strategic consideration, you represent your own platform of influence, whether you realize it or not. Make sure those people know what you are up to!

4. **Website** — A no-brainer. This should be the landing spot for people, which can be utilized as a sharable platform and include all mediums (quality video, audio, photography, graphics, branding, etc.).

5. **Social Media** — This one should also go without noting. But, make sure you are plugged into the social media platforms that your particular audience/people groups engage.

6. **Other Outlets** — Don't miss any opportunity to share the collective vision with others. News, blogs, podcasts, speaking opportunities, conferences, collateral materials, swag, etc. Know how your target audience gathers and shares information.

Financial Sustainability:

Financial sustainability stands alone as one of the single most apparent benchmarks for operational success. This is true for any business, organization, or movement. Starting a new project/program/initiative must involve a robust plan for financial sustainability.[5] Areas for consideration include:

1. **Startup Funds** — These are funds available from institutional or individual sources, including venture capitalist that specialize in nonprofit support.

2. **Personal Network** — Make sure you lean into your personal network. These are people who will invest in you because of their relationship with and belief in you. Give them an opportunity to make that investment.

3. **Granting Agencies** — There are a number of granting sources to which you can apply — foundations, granting organizations, local/

---

[5] Note: As you focus on financial sustainability, there must also be proper systems of financial accountability put into place. Remember, you and your team are accountable to your board, granting agencies, and community partners.

state/government programs, etc. Find those sources that align with your vision/mission and your programatic approach to positive social change.

4. **Donor Campaign and Fundraising** — Do not miss an opportunity for people both inside and outside of your organization to give. Make it easy for them to do so. There are various apps and online platforms that you can utilize.

5. **Social Enterprise** — At the core of your organization must be several alternative revenue streams, leaning into the social justice mission of the organization as a whole (e.g., coalitions, workforce development, job readiness, coffeehouse/restaurant, consignment/ thrift store, theater, art center, etc.).

6. **Donor Advised Funds/Endowments** — Donor advised funds are often overlooked in the efforts to cultivate financial sustainability. An endowment is beneficial to the giver and the receiver; income or a form of property can be given to an individual or organization.

Evaluation and Assessment:

It is an understatement to say that knowing when you are succeeding, and when you are not, is extremely important. Innovation breaks open new ways of interpreting metrics. Life will never be the same post-pandemic and this disruption has given way to rethinking how we engage one another, frame success, and determine the models that achieve it. Now is the time to evaluate our existing metrics (perceived or otherwise) and shift to new.

Like so many groups, we continually work to establish metrics that are derived within the cultural context. For us, this centers on community engagement through five cultural shifts that can give evidence of positive social change. Together, these shifts can reveal a practical way of contextual problem solving, while helping redefine what it looks like to create positive social change.

Examples of these shifts[6] include:

Fragmented Isolation >>>> To **Neighborhood Presence**

Consumer Posture >>>> To **Collaborative Participation**

Unrecognized Privilege >>>> To **Equitable Inclusion**

Scarcity Lens >>>> To **Abundant Ecology**

Toxic Charity >>>> To **Community Caring**

Remember, the old cliché, "what gets measured gets done" is true. If you don't measure outcomes, they won't be achieved. What change do you want to see? The above shifts move the organization from services "for" and "to" toward service "with" those in their community (core to an asset-based community development approach). This is an important pivot which might require the organization or team to rewire their thinking. A solid feedback loop is essential to maintaining a culture of innovation. Evaluation must happen internally and externally and must also identify both qualitative and quantitative data. Here are some things to consider when you are developing a feedback loop for evaluation and adjustments:

---

[6] These five shifts were developed by the Parish Collective (https://www.parishcollective.org).

1. **Establish a Culture of Listening** — A culture of listening welcomes feedback, approaching it with a posture of curiosity and holding it with open hands.

2. **Seek Feedback** — Hold regular meetings with your board, team, and staff and provide intentional opportunities for outside voices to give feedback.

3. **Gather Information** — Make sure that you are collecting information from across the spectrum of your plan.

4. **Analyze** — Process the feedback against the vision, mission, and value proposition. Make sure there is alignment.

5. **Make Changes** — Make the appropriate changes, based on evaluated feedback.

6. **Communicate** — Once changes have been made, make sure to share the "new," which reinforces a culture of listening.

Here it may be helpful to recall Eric Ries' build-measure-learn (in chapter 2) from *The Lean Startup*. which frames the feedback loop for a process of optimization.

To measure movement or success, you must establish **key performance indicators (KPIs)** that are contextual for your organization. Areas could include (but not be limited to) the following:

- Financial Sustainability/Fundraising and Development
- Programs and Services
- Human Capital (staff and volunteers)
- Marketing and Communications

- Outreach, Advocacy, and Policy
- Information Technology
- Risk Management and Governance
- Facilities and Capital projects, etc.

We will revisit more about KPIs and feedback loops in Chapter 15.

Remember, your **vital actions** are the most important tasks that have to happen to advance your mission. They will be directly informed by the strategic goals that advance the mission. Know explicitly what tasks must happen to move the organization forward and toward accomplishing the mission.

Discussion Questions for Vital Actions:

1. What will be your vital actions under the category of people?

2. What will be your vital actions under the category of communication plan?

3. What will be your vital actions under the category of financial sustainability?

4. What will be your vital actions under the category of evaluation and adjustments?

5. How will you create necessary feedback loops and establish key performance indicators?

CHAPTER 10
Vital Resources

Vital resources are the most important assets
required to make the business model work.
Building a safe space for everyone demands that we see
(from every angle) what everyone can bring to the equation. However,
many resources that are right in front of us are often overlooked.

As you and your organization collaborate with the community,
identifying your collective combination of assets is critical. This intersects
the work of Asset-Based Community Development (ABCD) and begins
by categorizing your resources. Think through and list your **vital
resources**, based on the following four categories:

1. **Physical Resources** — These resources are made up of land,
   buildings, property, and equipment — tangible items — that can
   be utilized to accomplish the mission.

2. **Intellectual Resources** — These resources are intangible
   resources such as contact lists, know-how/expertise, brands,
   copyrights, established partnerships, revenue streams, etc.

3. **Human Resources** — These resources represent the leaders,
   team members, employees, volunteers, teachers, coordinators,
   managers, organizations, etc., that partner (or could partner)
   with your company toward accomplishing the mission.

4. **Financial Resources** — These resources are the most apparent and include cash, stocks, and lines of credit.

Identifying your resources, particularly by exploring each of these four categories, will reveal assets you may have not considered in your planning process. There is no way to leverage an asset that you don't recognize as having some contributing value.

In our American context, the idea that we are to provide services "to" and "for" others has driven a programatic approach for community engagement. However, today, in a growing individualistic America where consumer culture flourishes, it is more and more important to focus on deepening relationships beyond the transactional. Again, this means we must shift from "to" and "for" toward "with" and "by," so that collaboration is central.

Community organizing, which we touched on in Chapter 6, gives way to the kind of listening that must happen in our contexts and forces us to test our assumptions and identify need. Moving away from a transactional approach, what if we were able to join with our neighbors to build lasting change and improve the circumstances of people's lives? This is where ABCD provides new opportunities for all of us to live out the idea of caring community.

This approach to community development was birthed by John McKnight and John Kretzmann while they were at Northwestern University. At the core of McKnight and Kretzmann's ABCD approach rests three important facts: **1) everyone has gifts; 2) everyone has something to contribute; and 3) everyone cares about something and that passion is his or her motivation to act**. Rather than seeing or treating others as consumers, an ABCD approach moves people from a

Photo credit: My Life Through a Lens, unsplash.com.

passive posture to an active collaborator. Therefore, the ABCD approach begins from and looks for the gifts and strengths (assets) people have to contribute.

In order to shift from a scarcity mindset, which in ABCD terms is deficit-based (and where needs are identified), ABCD identifies, pulls together, and builds upon strengths. The idea that "we are better together" recognizes that a position of abundance (contributed resources) opens new possibilities. Considering the five shifts pointed out in Chapter 9, this moves us from a scarcity lens to abundant ecology.

The Tamarack Institute offers eight helpful touchstones in the work of Asset-Based Community Development. You can start by asking these three questions: 1) **What can we do?** 2) **What do we need outside**

help with? 3) **What do we need outside agencies to do for us?** The Tamarack Institute's *eight touchstones*[7] to ABCD work are as follows:

1. **Establish a Community-building Team** — What people are good at discovering what others care about and where their assets can be used?

2. **Recruit/Empower a Community Organizer** — This is not someone who will set an agenda, but someone who is skilled and passionate about helping people organize.

*A great example of **ABCD** is the community development work of **Community Development for All People** in Columbus, Ohio. Check them out.*

3. **Host Community Conversations** — Create opportunities for diverse conversations to take place, focused not on "deliverables" but on mutual discovery.

4. **Engage Community Groups and Organizations** — Clubs, associations, and informal groups offer great capacity towards community building.

5. **Build Connections and Social Interaction** — Connectors and organizers are to create meaningful interactions, not just plan events.

---

[7] Tamarack Institute for Community Engagement, Waterloo, Ontario, Canada, "Asset-Based Community Development at a glance" — For more details on these touchstones, and an overview of ABCD offered by the Tamarack Institute, check out the following link: https://www.tamarackcommunity.ca/library/guide-asset-based-community-development-at-a-glance

6. **Inspire Vision and Plan for the Future** — Once trusting relationships have begun to form, look to the future to imagine together what the community could look like (e.g., ten years from now).

7. **Implement Change** — Take action and next steps to work towards your shared vision for the future — positive social change in your context.

8. **Foster Celebration** — Throughout the process, take joy in every positive development, in each person's gifts, and the effort they invest. Believe in and encourage each other.

Identifying your **vital resources** help to set a foundation for your work. To do so, you have to look around and take inventory of what you already have; those important pieces you have access to that are often overlooked. An ABCD approach will help you integrate what you have, while also opening up new possibilities and partnerships that advance the mission.

Discussion Questions and Considerations for Vital Resources:

1. Utilize the four categories (physical, intellectual, human, and financial) in order to think through and list your assets.

2. Considering these vital resources, how will they inform your curiosity when you are conducting one-to-one meetings and/or conducting deep listening in your context?

3. What will be your plan for an Asset-Based Community Development approach in your context?

4. How will more BIPOC and other leaders from the margins lead community development processes?

CHAPTER 11
Vital Partners

Vital partners represent the network of partners that help make the business model work. These relationships are essential to its development and effectiveness. They are especially important when building capacity — optimizing your strategic plan. It involves understanding economy of scale and encouraging risk-taking innovation, while limiting exposure to financial risk and pivoting as necessary.

Partnerships are formed for many reasons. They can be for efficiency, risk reduction, to leverage aligned strategies, or even to acquire valuable resources. Vital partners can advance your cause by leaning into expertise that may not yet exist on your team or within your organization or project scope. Why try to reinvent something that another organization is already doing well, when collaboration may be an immediate possibility? You can accomplish more with vital partners, while they also can help you navigate uncharted waters.

Coming out of our last chapters on Vital Actions and Vital Resources, and the overview of asset-based community development, there are essentially four questions when considering partnerships.

1. Who are your current vital partners?

2. Do you have any key suppliers that provide goods or services connected to your project/programs/initiatives?

Photo credit: Cytonn Photography, unsplash.com

3. Which vital actions are completed by these partners?

4. Which identified vital resources are actually provided by these partners?

Vital partners come in all forms of relationships. While some may be connected to your organization, others are born from connections established in your community — your target audience. In this way, you may think of partnerships as inside partners (directly related to the organization) and external partners (those autonomous organizations that are part of the heartbeat of your community).

When we review our areas of consideration for vital actions (from Chapter 9), there are four compartments to think through: **People, Communication Plan, Financial Sustainability**, and **Evaluation and Assessments**. Each of these categories also provides us ways to identify existing partners or those vital partnerships that are needed. As this relates to your **Vital Actions** work, some examples to process of **vital partners** include:

*Check out how **vital partners** can help create space, agency, and belonging for everyone in the community.*
***Everybody House**, in Twin Falls, Idaho and led by Buddy Gharring, is a great example of leveraged property and assets.*

People:

1. Is there a vital partner who will help you and your leaders/participants, become more culturally self-aware?

2. Is there a vital partner who specializes in community organizing?

3. Are there vital partners which directly align with the organization's mission?

4. Who are you engaging politically on the local, city, county, state, and national level?

Communication Plan:

1. If they exist, describe the vital partner contributions to your communication plan?

2. Who is tending your communication strategies?

3. Describe the vital partner(s) in the area of news outlets, blogs, conferences, etc.

Financial Sustainability:

1. Who is providing your startup funding?

2. What granting agencies align with your vision/mission? And what programs do they support?

3. Who are your vital partners (startup, operations, suppliers, volunteers/employees, etc.) helping operate your social enterprise?

Evaluation and Assessments:

1. Is there a vital partner who helps (or can help) define metrics?

2. Who helps monitor success and how it is defined?

3. Remember, "what gets measured gets done." What are you measuring? (again, key performance indicators (KPIs) will be discussed more in Chapter 15).

These questions, and others you will uncover, will help you identify existing and needed partners, as they relate to operations.

When you do the same examination, based on your vital resources, you will also add to the list of existing and/or needed collaborators. These are classified in the compartments of **Physical**, **Intellectual**, **Human**, and **Financial** resources. Some examples connected to your vital resources and ABCD work include the following:

Physical Resources:

1. Is there a vital partner with land or a building which may be available for use?

2. Is there a vital partner who can provide you with equipment (computers, office/area furniture, etc.)?

Intellectual Resources:

1. Is there a vital partner who can help with demographic research?

2. Is there a vital partner who can provide access to people lists?

3. Is there a vital partner with know-how that aligns with your vision/mission?

Human Resources:

1. Who are the other leaders that align with your vision/mission?

2. Who are your team members?

3. Who can volunteer time and energy?

4. What outside organizations can help you accomplish your goals?

Financial Resources:

1. Who is providing access to funding?

2. What other organizations could provide access to funding?

3. Is there a vital partner who provides an alternative revenue stream?

These questions, among others, can offer a needed perspective on your vital partners or those needed in support of your project.

For your project/programs/initiative to be successful, outside partners must be identified and invited into the work of community development in all areas. Strategic alliances, joint ventures, and intentional collaboration can make for a robust team of vital partners.

Discussion Questions and Considerations for Vital Partners:

1. Considering the vital actions and vital resources listed, how will you identify existing or potential vital partners?

2. Do all these identified or potential partners align with your vision and mission?

3. How many BIPOC partners or partners from the margins have you identified?

4. How will you evaluate what cultural perspectives are under or over represented to inform your identification process?

CHAPTER 12
Cost Structures

The **cost structures** represent all costs incurred to operate the organization. This building block helps you see the most important costs that are incurred while engaging the wider community through the strategies of your organization as a whole. These expenses can be calculated relatively easily, once your vital resources, vital actions, and vital partners have all been defined.

Your business model can be more cost-driven (a focus on keeping costs down), depending on which strategies are employed and when. This is where lean startup strategies, which leverage existing relationships, shared resources, and create space for the multiplication of leaders, are essential. This allows for initial growth and scalability.

The cost structure that shapes your budgeting process is closely related to the value proposition. Drilling down to the practical is incredibly important to producing valid numbers. You must be meticulous so that you don't under represent actual costs. How do you know what you need if you don't know the costs?

For example, in the for-profit lane, let's say you are making widgets. And, you have a target sale price that's based on market research and focus group interaction with your product (what you learn people will pay). In order to meet a sale price that would appropriately represent the value proposition for a particular target audience, you have to know your costs. Keeping cost down means a close look at manufacturing contracts, supply chains, marketing, and point-of-sale promotions. This helps you see whether you can feasibly make the widget and a profit. There has to be enough margin to cover all your costs, while creating financial capacity for more impact. Cost structures become the basis for establishing the necessary revenue streams that allow for sustainability and scalability. Costs inform price/financial capacity.

Through a social entrepreneurship approach, the work you have to do involves much translation. Don't get so bogged down that you lose focus on the vision/mission. Remember, you have to see this work through a social change lens. This is an added level of discovery that delineates between a for-profit and a non-profit effort designed to subvert consumer culture rather than capitalize on it.

Now that you have done some initial work on your vital actions, vital resources, and vital partners, you can begin to more closely understand your costs. Like building a house, keeping cost down — without completely sacrificing quality and efficiency — is important to value assessment and financing for the builder or potential home owner. Businesses define cost structures in four categories. Each of these categories helps you frame and think about your operating costs. They are as follows:

1. **Cost-driven** — Remember, cost-driven structures are designed to keep expenses down. Non profit organizations can create cost savings through streamlined operations, particularly within social enterprise projects. There are two ways this is represented: **Economies of scale** and **Economies of scope**. Economies of scale represent the cost savings as a business grows. As the business grows it can benefit from volume discounts, which result in lower product costs. Economies of scope represent cost

Photo credit: Tierra Mallorca, <u>unsplash.com</u>

savings that a company experiences as the business expands its market share. Market leaders can leverage their operation to expand product lines. A cost-driven approach can also be achieved in your organization, by embracing lean startup strategies, keeping cost low in the beginning. It is especially important to embrace lean operational strategies with a nonprofit, in order to channel as much resources to programatic impact.

2. **Value-driven** — Value-driven cost structures rest on providing more value through premium products or services. Apple is a great example of value-driven cost structures, as they leverage their products to gain consumers who value quality, performance, and the brand more than price. This strategy builds customers and brand loyalty through perceived value. You

can think about value-driven cost structures as they relate to excellence in what is offered through your new project. This directly relates to how the value proposition is offered to your target audience, in all forms.

3. **Fixed costs** — Fixed costs are those cost that do not change with the volume of products or services sold. Examples include salaries, taxes, interest, insurance, lease payments, utilities, etc. These costs do not typically change over the span of an agreement. For the purpose of launching a new project or new social enterprise, calculate your known fixed cost connected to your first year for a business plan, and three to five years out, for your strategic plan.

4. **Variable costs** — In the business world, variable costs change based on proportion to production output. If there is a decrease or an increase in production, the costs of that production can decrease or increase. Examples of variable costs are things such as commissions, shipping, labor rate per item produced, and supplies. If we use our bakery example from earlier, the more loaves of bread you bake, plus the cost of labor (the person baking), variable costs of baking the bread increases. There will be certain costs that can be controlled more easily than fixed costs, in order to maintain financial sustainability. This will primarily relate to the social enterprise. You must consider how variable costs affect program development, implementation, and impact with your nonprofit.

I cannot emphasize enough the importance of understanding your cost structures. The majority of businesses fail in the first three years of existence, primarily because of a lack of understanding of their costs and what it actually takes to deliver their value proposition. Figuring out your **vital actions**, **vital resources**, and **vital partners** makes forecasting costs and revenue for operations more accurate.

Discussion Questions and Considerations for Cost Structures:

1. Considering your emerging business model, list out your anticipated costs based on the preceding four categories.

2. Is your business model more cost-driven or value-driven?

3. Where are the areas you can keep costs low in the early phases of development?

4. What things might you get free or receive in-kind in order to keep costs down?

5. How might you think and see cost structures through a social change lens?

	January	February	March	April	May	June	July	August	September	October	November	December	Year End
Revenue:													
· Startup Funding	7,100	7,100	7,100	7,100	7,100	7,100	7,100	7,100	7,100	7,100	7,100	7,100	85,200
· Grants	20,000	7,500	7,500	7,500	7,500	7,500	20,000	7,500	7,500	7,500	7,500	7,500	115,000
· Giving	6,000	6,200	8,000	12,000	9,200	6,200	5,500	4,800	6,000	9,200	10,000	15,000	98,100
· Social Enterprise	2,200	3,550	3,725	6,700	8,000	8,200	8,500	8,900	9,150	10,050	10,750	12,400	92,125
Gross Income:	35,300	24,350	26,325	33,300	31,800	29,000	41,100	28,300	29,750	33,850	35,350	42,000	390,425
Operating Expenses:													
· Salaries & Wages	10,541	10,541	10,541	10,541	10,541	10,541	10,541	10,541	10,541	10,541	10,541	10,541	126,492
· Professional Services	1,500	1,500	1,500	1,500	1,500	1,500	1,500	1,500	1,500	1,500	1,500	1,500	18,000
· Programs	6,000	5,000	5,000	5,500	6,000	7,000	7,000	7,500	7,500	7,500	9,000	12,500	85,500
· Rent/Lease	5,000	5,000	5,000	5,000	5,000	5,000	5,000	5,000	5,000	5,000	5,000	5,000	60,000
· Equipment Rental	1,200	1,200	1,200	1,200	1,200	1,200	1,200	1,200	1,200	1,200	1,200	1,200	14,400
· Insurance	500	150	150	150	150	150	500	150	150	150	150	150	2500
· Utilities	650	725	600	550	475	475	475	475	475	550	600	650	6700
· Office Supplies	900	200	200	200	200	200	200	200	200	200	200	200	3100
· Marketing/Advertising	5,000	2,500	2,500	2,500	4,000	2,500	2,500	2,500	2,500	5,000	5,000	6,500	43,000
· Travel	1,500	1,500	1,500	1,500	1,500	1,500	1,500	1,500	1,500	1,500	1,500	1,500	18,000
· Professional Expenses	500	500	500	500	500	500	500	500	500	500	500	500	6000
Total Operating Expenses:	33,291	28,816	28,691	29,141	31,066	30,566	30,916	31,066	31,066	33,641	35,191	40,241	383,692
Net Profit:	2,009	-4,466	-2,366	4,159	734	-1,566	10,184	-2,766	-1,316	209	159	1,759	6,733

Fig. 1.5. Example of Cost Structure categories as presented in a financial projection.

CHAPTER 13
Revenue Streams

The **revenue streams** represent the funds generated in the process of reaching and co-creating with the market segments/target audience. Obviously, your revenue streams must be higher than your cost structures to maintain financial sustainability and scalability. Customers are essential for the success of businesses, whether the businesses are offering products or services. For the work of launching a new project, program, or social enterprise, relationships with people and organizations are the necessary drivers.

As you consider the value proposition, and how it is offered and communicated to the market segments/target audiences, there are a few leading questions to address. Additionally, your cost structures dictate your revenue streams. As these are identified, think through the following questions:

1. How does value translate in the activity of giving or making a transaction (through a social enterprise) with your target audience?

2. How do they prefer to pay/give?

3. What percentage does each revenue stream add to the bottomline?

4. How might your cost structures be adjusted accordingly?

Revenue streams can be transactional, one-time gifts, or recurring payments as a part of a larger giving campaign. In order to support the

*Social enterprise, as an alternative **revenue stream**, should come from a discovered need in the community, by way of deep listening. Check out how **ReVillage**, led by Erika Spaet in Bend, Oregon is helping provide affordable, equitable childcare to families.*

kinds of strategies required for your new project or social enterprise, you will need to develop multiple revenue streams. Considering what I have already presented in chapter 9, which focused on vital actions, let's expand the list of examples under the necessary actions related to financial sustainability.

1.**Startup Funds** — While these funds represent an advance on future viability, you still need to list out all possible sources.

-Individual large donors

-Venture capitalists for nonprofit work

2.**Personal Network** — Again, these are people who believe in you and will invest in you and the difference you desire to make in the world. Some of these sources will continue to give well beyond the startup phase.

- Family
- Friends
- Associates
- Other networked relationships

3. **Granting Organizations** — Again, find those sources that align with your vision/mission and your programatic approach to positive social change.

    - Granting organizations that align with your vision/mission

    - Organizations focused on charitable giving

    - Other sources

4. **Donor Campaign and Fundraising** — You need to develop multiple opportunities for people to give. Don't miss developing this passive outlet.

    - Online giving

    - Giving by text

    - Onsite transactions (Square, Intuit Go Payment, etc.)

    - Annual giving campaign/commitment

5. **Social Enterprise** — Social enterprises can include a number of revenue streams, which have already been previously listed. But the number of transaction opportunities needs to be identified for your specific model.

    - Products

    - Services

    - Rental/lease payments

    - Usage fees

    - Subscription fees

    - Advertising opportunities for non-competing entities

6. **Endowments/Foundations** — These often overlooked sources of revenue, which align with the vision/mission, should be pursued. This

Photo credit: Pepi Stojanovski,

includes opportunities to either set up an endowment for investment income or access the funds of an existing endowment operating as a granting agency.

- Large donors
- Established endowments
- Educational institutions
- Service-oriented organizations

Making an exhaustive list of all the possible revenue streams is important to building a realistic and accurate budget. The importance of flexibility cannot be stated enough. Ongoing adjustments will be the norm. Remember, cash flow is the lifeblood of any successful business. Without strategies for how money flows in and out, you are sunk.

Discussion Questions and Considerations for Revenue Streams:

1. What agencies or institutions can you approach for startup funds?

2. Build an exhaustive list of people based on your personal network.

3. Who are the granting agencies you could approach with a request?

4. How will you build robust giving opportunities in support of your new project?

    a. What are the different modes of payment you will employ that matches your particular group's preferences?

5. What kind of social enterprise makes sense in your context?

    a. What benefits will help customers make buying decisions?

6. What will be your plan for setting up or accessing endowments?

7. How does your cash flow pencil out? Or, does your cash flow meet your model?

SECTION 3:
Pulling it All Together

This final section offers an overview of how to put together your strategic plan, highlights the importance of feedback loops, and showcases additional resources to help in your planning process.

CHAPTER 14
Constructing Your
Strategic Plan

Now that you have worked through all the building blocks of the process, you should have the necessary information critical to developing a robust and flexible plan. Incorporating the concept of "chaordic tension" (discussed in chapter 2) is important and will help cultivate the successful union of innovation and the organization. Again, most new initiatives/projects don't fail because of a lack of funding or staffing. They fail because of poor or missing research, strategy, or planning.

While the planning process can be intimidating and take a significant investment of time, the benefits are boundless. And, to embody risk-taking practices, while limiting financial disaster, demands that you plan and prepare. Remaining in the tension, between innovation and the demand for order, forces you to new ways of navigating risk. As you push for calculated decisions, you must hold space for adaptability in your plan. In ever-shifting culture, where the unexpected will rear its ugly head (such as a pandemic), your plan must not only allow for pivots, but also anticipate them.

Depending on the stage of your project/program/initiative or social enterprise, the process of developing a plan should push you in two directions. The two types of plans to consider are the **business plan** and the **strategic plan**. A business plan is a type of strategic plan but its primary purpose is to introduce a business idea, and the key players, to

Photo credit: Kelly Sikkima, unsplash.com

garner funding, and to explain operations in detail. In the work of starting a new project/program/initiative or social enterprise, a business plan outlines the early stages of your business model, with specific emphasis on the foundation of your first year. The business plan also showcases the expertise of the founders, as investor confidence in leadership is just as important (if not more) than the innovative idea you are trying to get off the ground. Finally, having done your appropriate homework, you should be able to create realistic financial projections.

Separately, the strategic plan picks up where the business plan leaves off, covering a period of three to five years. The purpose of a strategic plan is to implement and oversee the strategy of a business or organization that is starting to grow, get traction, or scale its model. This plan brings focus and action to move the organization closer to defined goals. Prioritizing vital resources and vital actions, and expanding vital partnerships move the organization toward revenue growth and measured success (or ROI), with sustainability and scalability as a driver. Think of a strategic plan as the playbook for the organization, which keeps the team on the same page and moves everyone in a specific direction. And, as a part of the necessary evaluation and adjustment process, the strategic plan can be modified as needed.

> *"The **Strategic Plan** is the playbook that defines, maps, and/or guides the organization through its strengths and challenges, in order to achieve its vision, mission, goals, and sustainable successes over the years ahead."*
> *—Sustineri Group, Inc.*

In thinking through the arc of a strategic plan, Professor John M. Bryson,[8] who serves as the McNight Presidential Professor of Planning and Public Affairs at Hubert H. Humphrey School of Public Affairs, University of Minnesota, begins with the following questions:

1. What is the situation you are addressing?

2. What do you want to do?

3. How are you going to do it?

4. What would be the result if you accomplished what you want to do?

These framing questions can help you shape a coherent narrative that links purpose and passion. It's important to help your team and other close stakeholders to clearly understand where the organization is

---

[8] John M. Bryson authored *Strategic Planning for Public and Nonprofit Organizations*, which is accessible online here: https://books.google.com/books/about/Strategic_Planning_for_Public_and_Nonpro.html?id=2JJFDwAAQBAJ.

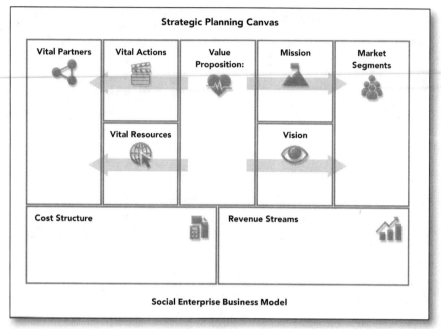

Figure 1.2

headed. This is how a plan shifts people into the practical steps/actions that push the organization toward its goals. Think of these questions as touchstones as you work through the arc of your planning process.

The Sections of Your Plan

There are a number of sections in a traditional strategic plan. For the purpose of practical implementation, I have customized the following headings for a new project/program/initiative or social enterprise. This is one way to categorize the content and data you have pulled together through this process. The headings are as follows:

- Executive summary *(Note: created last but listed first)*
- Vision statement

- Mission statement
- DEI Strategy
- Market segments analysis
- SWOT Analysis (Strengths, Weaknesses, Opportunities, Threats)
- Strategic goals
- Marketing/advertising/communication plan
- Community impact and development
- Metrics and evaluation
- Financial projections/budget

Constructing Your Strategic Plan

You've done the hard work of research, leadership identification, collaboration, and deep listening. You should now have all the necessary information and initial answers in order to begin constructing your strategic plan (you addressed all these questions through the Strategic Planning Process of Section 2). To help organize this information, you can utilize the outline below.

1. **Executive Summary** — A good executive summary is clear and concise and does not contain everything you will layout in your entire plan (*NOTE: The executive summary should be created at the end of the process, after you have completed your research, analysis, and planning, so that it offers a concise summary of your overall strategic plan*). It's a one or two page compelling snapshot of your new project/social enterprise that is used to capture interest and convey passion to the reader.

   - What is the identified problem or need?

- Who is your audience?
- What is your elevator speech?
- What is your launch budget?
- What is your revenue forecast?
- What is your funding sources or funding needs?
- Who is on your team and what are their collective qualifications?

2. **Vision Statement** — Your vision statement, or *what can be*, is a concise version of your elevator speech.
   - What is the vision statement you created with people from your target audience?
   - What is compelling and inspiring?

3. **Mission Statement** — Your mission statement, or *what we are compelled to do*, is a contextualized version of the mission.
   - What is the purpose of your organization?
   - How would you translate the mission statement for your context?
   - How is equity and justice being addressed?

4. **DEI Strategy** — Your DEI strategy must take into consideration the need to deconstruct a colonial mindset.
   - What is your plan to utilize an equity lens (self, team and organization)?
   - What is your plan for meeting new people and listening to place?
   - Where does difference convene in your context?

- How will you decenter white or other privileged voices?
- What issues disproportionally impact vulnerable communities and what movements will you engage?
- How will you cultivate cultural humility and resilience for the work of justice?
- How will you know you are succeeding?

5. **Market Segments Analysis** — Describe the makeup of the target audiences/market segments and all that you have learned about the community.

   - What are the demographics?
   - What have you learned from BIPOC community members or others closer to the margins that inform your strategies?
   - Describe your most significant one-to-one listening sessions.
   - What is the identified problem(s) or need(s) or opportunities?
   - How would you assess the risk tolerance of your audience?
   - What outside organizations/groups have you connected with that align with the vision/mission?

6. **SWOT Analysis** — Conduct a SWOT Analysis to help you develop a solid strategic approach for your organization. It is important to include different perspectives and stakeholders in this examination.

   - What are the strengths of your organization?
     - What do you do well?
   - What are the weaknesses of your organization?
     - What areas need improvement?
   - What are the opportunities for your organization?

- What opportunities exist within your market segments that you can benefit from?
- What are the threats your organization might face?
  - What factors beyond your control could put your organization at risk or in jeopardy?

7. **Strategic Goals** — There should be a number of goals set, which come directly out of the identified mission of your organization. The following example questions can help you define your strategic goals for each practice (you may have your own core practices that align with your values, and if so, consider those. The following are examples, based on practices highlight for our organization and work).

1. Positive Social Change (Value Proposition)
   - What have you learned about your market segments (characteristics) that would shape the language you use to express value?
   - What value does your organization offer to improve the quality of life of others?
   - How do the people groups gather their information, communicate with, and engage one another?

2. Innovation and Entrepreneurship (Market Segments, Vision, and Mission)
   - What new things do you want to explore or pioneer?
   - Name the positive risks that need to happen for your project to be successful.
   - How can your new project bring difference together?
   - What is your plan for collaborating with others?

- How will your understanding of community and culture help shift your organization from "for" and "to" toward "with" and "by" those in your community?
- What do your feedback loops look like and how will they inform pivots?

3. Social impact and Growth (Vital Actions, Vital Resources, Vital Partners)

   - What social justice initiatives align with your project/programs/ initiatives or social enterprise?
   - What is your plan for identifying and developing leaders?
   - Who are your vital partners?
   - What vital resources are you able to leverage?
   - What social enterprise or alternative revenues streams have you identified or developed?
   - Describe your financial sustainability plan.

*Your **strategic goals** are directly connected to the mission of your organization and they shape the programs you develop with your community. Check out the **Latino Network** in Portland, Oregon and how their programs provide agency for community members to participate in the decisions that affect their lives and the lives of their families.*

111

Take these answers (or those from your identified practices) and formulate clear goals. For examples, refer to Chapter 8, page 74-75.

8. **Marketing/Advertising/Communication Plan** — Depending on your business model, you will need to think through your marketing, advertising, and communication strategies. Today, information is available instantly and you have to show how your new project or social enterprise is plugged into those channels of communication.

   - How is the value proposition communicated through the aesthetics of images, words, brands, and spaces?
   - Consumers are conditioned to look for quality and the best value. How will this inform or subvert the interpretation of the value proposition?
     - Name strategies
   - How will your understanding of a consumer perspective help you subvert skepticism and embrace integrity?
   - What are your strategic talking points?
     - List out the appropriate talking points for everyone at every level of the organization (they may be different)
   - Who is managing and updating your website and social media platforms?
     - Name the department and/or individuals and how their expertise will be deployed
   - Explain your social media strategies.
     - Name the platforms, why they align with your mission, and how you will leverage them
   - Describe the vital partner contributions to your communication plan (news outlets, blogs, conferences, etc.).

9. **Community Impact and Development** — This represents the proposed change or solution to the identified problem(s), need(s), or opportunities in your community. Your vital resources play a significant role in this work. Utilizing ABCD strategies helps move your organization from a passive posture to an active collaborator. This approach moves people from a scarcity mindset to the notion that "we are better together," leveraging gifts and strengths.

   - How is the wider community represented in your initiatives?
   - How are BIPOC or other voices from the margins leading community development initiatives?
   - What vital assets have you identified (physical, intellectual, human, financial, economic, knowledge, network, innovation, etc.)?
   - Who are your vital partners, and how are you collaborating with them? What are they providing that you cannot?
   - What is your overall ABCD approach?

10. **Metrics and Evaluation** — Metrics and evaluation help guide our strategies — they show if success is being achieved or goals reached. This demands an organizational culture of innovation, where flexibility allows for adjustments and pivots.

   - What are the metrics you will utilize to gauge success?
   - How will your metrics align with your determined values and practices?
   - Describe your process for evaluation and assessment (feedback loop).
   - Indicate to whom you are accountable.

- What are the key performance indicators (KPIs) you have identified?

  - For examples of KPIs, review Chapter 15, page 122.

11. **Financial Projections/Budget** — Having worked with both the delivery (market segments, vision, mission) and operational (vital actions, vital resources, vital partners) sides of your business model, you should have the necessary numbers to represent your cost structures and revenue streams.

    - What are the categories of your cost structures?
    - What are the numbers that represent your cost structures?
    - What are the categories of your revenue streams?
    - What are the numbers that make up your revenue streams?
    - Create your financial projections/budget, showing how you will manage the cashflow of your new project or social enterprise over a one-year period (for a business plan) or a three- to five-year period (for your strategic plan). See Figure 1.5.
    - What are your projected income and expenses over the designated timeline(s)?

Tips for Writing Your Plan

After spending the necessary time on research, as framed through the Strategic Planning Process, the last thing you want to do is produce a plan that you don't actually use to guide the organization's strategies or operations. Put in the time so that your plan is a robust, flexible roadmap that gives you and your organization the best possible shot at achieving the identified goals. Here are a few tips in writing your plan:

1. **Appropriate Voices** — Involve the appropriate voices from your team and your context to support the writing and constructing process.

2. **Be Clear** — In your writing, be clear and concise. Long explanations can cause those following the roadmap to get confused or misunderstand the processes altogether.

3. **Put in the Time** — The planning process takes time. Do not take shortcuts. Put in the necessary effort and leave no stone unturned.

4. **Don't Ignore it** — Do not ignore what your business/strategic plan tells you. Why would you take the time to invest in the planning process only to put in on the shelf and ignore what it is telling you?

Discussion and Questions for Constructing Your Strategic Plan:

1. No more questions. It's time to pull everything together from the Strategic Planning Process into a clear, concise, flexible plan. Get started, now!

CHAPTER 15
The Necessity of
a Feedback Loop

In chapter 9, we briefly discussed the importance of a solid feedback loop in maintaining a culture of innovation. Innovation is about taking advantage of shifts and reimagining new ways forward. Remember, the evaluation process must be both internal and external. The list for consideration that I previously shared can help define your process of evaluation and adjustment.

1. Establish a culture of listening

2. Seek feedback

3. Gather information

4. Analyze

5. Make changes

6. Communicate

These steps can overlay multiple evaluative processes in your new project or social enterprise, creating a necessary process of optimization.

Beyond the basic pattern shown on the strategic planning canvas (*see Figure 1.4 on page 31*), there are other ways to engage the canvas/ process related to feedback loops. We can highlight these by looking at the **delivery** side (**market segments, vision**, and **mission**) and the **operational** side (**vital actions, vital resources**, and **vital partners**) of the process. This allows for four additional process loops within the business model that can assist in evaluating and adjusting specific areas of your strategic plan.

Delivery Side Feedback Loops

On the **delivery** side of the process (the right side of the Strategic Planning Process), it is important to open up communication channels for deep listening and feedback. When you engage the three primary blocks of the delivery side of the process model (**market segments, vision**, and **mission**), you are able to continuously track how 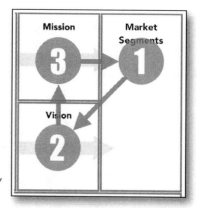 the value proposition is permeating community engagement. This smaller loop within the larger process enables continuous deep listening with people groups (**market segments**) and needed refinement of the **vision**, and helps adjust/align the **mission**. Maintaining a culture of listening allows for feedback/evaluation to influence necessary change sooner. If you represent power and privilege, you will need to be intentional about creating safe space for feedback from non-dominant cultures. Consider your position as a leader or leadership team in creating your feedback loops.

If you expand this loop to also include revenue streams, ongoing evaluation of alternative revenue streams and expansion remain directly connected to what is happening in or emerging from the wider

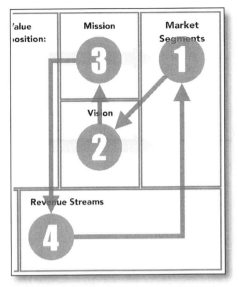

community. Revenue is generated through direct and indirect connection and collaboration with your target audiences. If you are not intentional about monitoring this interaction, you will miss necessary adjustments and/or new opportunities. How is your particular audience continuing to speak into the vision, participating and aligning with the mission, and what new opportunities might this interaction bring in the form of new revenue?

Operational Side Feedback Loops

Likewise, the **operational** side of the process (left side of the Strategic Planning Process) presents feedback loops that continue to inform sustainability and scalability. What is learned from the delivery side of the process will continue to inform, reshape, and even redefine the **operational** side (**vital actions, vital resources**, and **vital partners**). In this way, relationships established through community engagement can move to collaboration that helps grow the movement and increase community impact. **Vital actions** are identified through the **market segments, vision**, and **mission** loop, then inform ongoing identification of **vital resources**, before informing **vital partners**. If you engage this feedback loop as a part of the **operational** side, informed by the **delivery** side (community engagement data and emerging opportunities), your new project or social enterprise can refine its operational standards in order to scale appropriately.

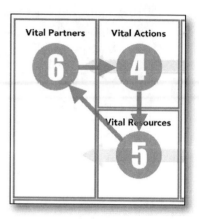

Just like the previous example on the **delivery** side, if you expand your **operational** loop (**vital actions**, **vital resources**, and **vital partners**) to include **cost structures**, this will identify any cost increases and opportunities to streamline work/production, and allow for improvement of operational efficiency. As new opportunities emerge through engaging the target audience, the idea is to increase revenue without increasing costs (remember the concept of economies of scale and economies of scope from chapter 12). If you do not monitor what is happening on the operational side, you could see disproportionate increases in costs without increased revenue. Remember, cash flow is the lifeblood of any business; therefore, managing it is vital to your continued success.

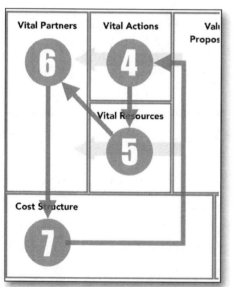

If you do not lean into a process of optimization that allows for evaluation and assessment, you will not have a culture of innovation within your organizational structure. This is the only way to make good of the tension and the ebb and flow within your strategic approach. This is how your

*Being able to **measure your impact** is critical to creating positive social change. Check out how **Peacehaven Community Farm**, in Whitsett, North Carolina, is growing vegetables and growing people in measurable way.*

organization can embrace the idea of "chaordic tension."

Metrics & Key Performance Indicators (KPIs)

H. Thomas Johnson, Accounting historian and Professor of Business Administration at Portland State University, is frequently quoted on the topic of metrics. He says, *"Perhaps what you measure is what you get. More likely, what you measure is all you'll get. What you don't (or can't) measure is lost."* Johnson's quote is the source for the old cliché mentioned earlier in chapter 9 — "what gets measured gets done." And it's true; as is the Peter Drucker attributed quote, "You can't manage what you don't measure."

Clearly, measuring progress (or the lack thereof) toward stated goals is a primary driver in how we deploy, support, resource, and direct employees toward completing the organization's mission. Knowing what to measure is critical and often changes as the social, political, historical, and consumer landscape shifts. This can make metrics a moving target, which demands tending on a regular basis. It also means you must define the indicators that point toward success and then measure the progress.

A key performance indictor (KPI)[9] is a quantifiable measurement that is used to evaluate the success of an organization, its employees, or teams in achieving the stated goals of performance. In the work we lead, our team has developed both qualitative and quantitative output indicators under the practices of diversity, equity, and inclusion; innovation and entrepreneurship; and social impact and growth, which represent the theory of change mentioned earlier in the book.

For instance, for **qualitative** outputs, examples under the practices previously shared are as follows *(Note: These are leading examples and not exhaustive)*:

- Positive Social Change: *Active in antiracism (and "isms") throughout the community*
- Innovation and Entrepreneurship: *Asset-based community development is identified and at work in the wider community*
- Social impact and Growth: *There are identified social enterprise supporting alternative revenue for sustainable community engagement*

For instance, for **quantitative** outputs, examples under the three practices are as follows:

- Positive Social Change: *Greater than 60% of leadership team represents diversity (who is not historically represented)*
- Innovation and Entrepreneurship: *Public calendar of at least 3 monthly community events in operation with circulation of more than 50 active participants*
- Social impact and Growth: *120% of budget coming through social enterprise, fundraising, and individual donor giving*

---

[9] See examples of KPIs area examples of an organization on page 74-75.

Based on your named strategic goals, develop realistic measurements of each category in your organization. If you do not name those key performance indicators, no one in your organization will know if they are meeting the expectations of success and you and your team will not be able to evaluate and adjust appropriately. There can be a number of KPIs based on your organization's business model. Remember to be very specific when defining these indicators. They should be very specific actionable and accurate metrics that indicate quantifiable progress meeting your goals.

Discussion Questions and Considerations for the Necessity of a Feedback Loop:

1. Identify the areas in your business model where feedback loops will be important?

2. How will you utilize this process of evaluation and adjustments to keep moving toward sustainability and scalability?

3. Name the areas of your organization where KPIs need to be named and measured.

4. Develop specific metrics that will indicate the expectations and progress toward strategic goals.

CHAPTER 16
A Final Reflection

That original question from my father — "How are you going to pay for it?" — continues to provide the entry point for my approach to strategic planning today. What I have provided in this book represents a creative approach to cultivating positive social change, through integrated practices of community engagement. I believe this work is vital and it can lead us to embody Lilla Watson's words, *"If you have come here to help me, you are wasting your time. But if you have come here because your liberation is bound up with mine, then let us work together."* Those words have been a source of grounding and inspiration for me.

While most of my career has focused on nonprofit management, my entrepreneurial spirit has been a driving force when it comes to problem solving. Having an idea that might make a difference is only the first step — we can produce hundreds of ideas. But, implementation and execution are key. Many tasks need to be addressed to cultivate positive social change within the community or region you serve. This must be rooted in curiosity and collaboration.

Remember, most businesses do not fail because of lack of funding or staffing, but because of the lack of research, strategy, and planning. The notion of "chaordic tension" — the very real tug of war that exists between the desire for order and the necessity of chaos — must be given serious consideration. If innovation happens at the intersection of difference (and I believe it can), then creating an organizational culture that makes adequate space for this disruption is essential.

Great ideas can sometimes catch you completely by surprise. You never know what you might stumble into. Crazy notions and unexpected conversations can lead to the most unpredictable outcomes, providing much needed learnings in the process. It reminds me of the pitch I made to my dad (which I shared with you in the introduction). It prompted his response, "That sounds like something worth pursuing. How are you going to pay for it?" And that sets up the following closing story about that very idea.

An Unexpected Axion

A few seasons ago, my former business partner, Barry Steadman,[10] and I embarked on designing a new action-oriented brand and clothing line. This was the idea I shared with my dad. The venture represented one of the many startup businesses over the course of my prior career. To set the stage, there was a craze during these years for the No Fear® brand. It was so popular that the company set strict parameters on sales and distribution. If one store in a retail center (or geographic area) already had the rights to sell the apparel, then no other store (in the same area) could sell it. The movement grew so big that No Fear® started opening corporate owned stores, which carried exclusive merchandise that other outlets couldn't offer.

Looking through our entrepreneur lens, Barry and I saw an opportunity. If demand was this high, and stores were limited in their ability to carry the merchandise, then room for competition existed. What did we do? We developed a competing brand, of course. The logo mark we designed and branded was Kick Axion®; our response to the idea of

[10] To learn more about Barry, visit: http://sgcdesign.com.

having no fear. In short, it was like taking "kick ass" and smashing it together with "take action." With the substitution of an "X" for the "c" and "t" in "action," we had a pretty cool brand coming on the scene. Our advertising tagline was, "You have nothing to fear but fear itself," which was attributed to the 1933 Inaugural Address of Franklin D. Roosevelt and an intentional jab at No Fear®.

After developing a logo, and then testing the brand with a number of focus groups, we initiated designs for an apparel line. Our debut product offering would be suede leather bill denim baseball caps with the logo embroidered on the front, along with T-shirts and Henleys, revealing the logo embroidered on the front left breast, and a large silkscreened logo on the back. At the time, this combination of embroidered and silkscreened apparel was something No Fear® did not offer. This alone made Kick Axion® somewhat unique. All the products were offered in various color combinations of earth tones.

About six weeks before the Christmas buying season, we had what we believed was a nice mix of options that could be test marketed. I had a connection at a regional department store chain in the Southeast (like a Macy's) and decided to pitch our new Kick Axion® apparel line, armed only with drawings. We grossly underestimated the desire for an alternative option to No Fear® and the response was a jolting surprise. Not only did the company want the merchandise to test it in several of their stores, but they wanted it for their Christmas sales push in the young men's department.

With a rather large purchase order in hand, the adrenalin rush of the sell, and the shocking reality that we had to actually deliver, I rushed back to the office to act out a dramatic, full report for Barry. We held a commitment to a new brand, a significant order for multiple stores, a

Original Kick Axion® apparel logo from in-store pre-Christmas promo, circa 1994.

laundry list of instructions ranging from advertising parameters to price tag formats (including skew numbers, etc.), and less than six weeks to deliver. Mind you, we had not actually produced any of the merchandise; not even samples. We only had drawings — laser ink printouts, perfectly mounted on boards. After the excitement wore off and the high fives exhausted our adrenalin, we looked at each other as if to say, "How the hell are we going to pull this off?"

Appropriately, the scramble ensued. The search for shirt and hat manufacturers, registering the trademark in multiple categories, reviewing samples, working on apparel sales tags, branded size tags for the shirts, negotiating a tight timeline with suppliers, working out distribution and delivery, generating a premiere edition advertising campaign, living with a fixed price point (because we sold it based on drawings and not how much it would cost to produce), and working under the pressure of a ticking clock, was a wild ride I would never forget. Somehow, we were able to keep everything pointed in the right direction.

I will never forget the day before our required delivery to the distribution center. Barry and I were at my house with apparel stacked all over the living room. While Barry was cutting, spray mounting, and attaching sales tags to each piece, I was on the phone with my aunt, as she explained to me how to use her sewing machine. I had never plugged in a sewing machine to a power outlet, much less inserted thread bobbers or actually sewn with a machine.

We were able to get the apparel manufactured to our specifications. And we were able to get another company to create branded tags for the hats and shirts. What we couldn't make happen in time was getting the tags sewn into the hats and shirts. This is why at 10:30PM I was on the phone with my aunt, trying to prepare a sewing machine. It was comical! For the rest of the night and into the early morning hours, we hustled feverishly to get everything boxed up to specs, and neatly placed in a borrowed truck for delivery later that morning.

Did I say that we had grossly underestimated the desire for an alternative to No Fear®? That Christmas season, the participating department stores sold 52% of the merchandise in the first 48 hours it was placed on the racks. It was a record for this department store. Facing an extremely tight timeline and all kinds of obstacles, we actually pulled it off. This had to be what it felt like for Charles Dickens to deliver his bestseller *A Christmas Carol* in the same timeframe. Of all things, that's what I remember thinking.

What came of the Kick Axion® brand? Though the department store wanted repeat orders, we were pursued by a clothing company out of

California that manufactured skateboard apparel and accessories, and finally relented after numerous offers. I bought a car with part of my earnings and added to my bank account and investments. Then we moved on to the next impossible opportunity.

What is the point of this story? More often than we realize, new opportunities appear right in front of us. The timing feels perfect but there remains a number of unknowns. Moving from an idea to implementation and execution will always be an awesome adventure; one where new relationships are created, lessons are learned, processes are improved, strategy is modified, and results are achieved.

You must be willing to embrace the uncertainties that may be before you and learn to be OK with failure. Failing is not an issue. In fact, it is required for success to be achieved. Trying new things and learning what works and doesn't work rests at the center of improvement and progress. This is why feedback loops (creating space for learning, evaluating, and improving) are the optimizing process of embracing failure within your strategic plan.

Throughout my career (and since Kick Axion®) I have taken what I have learned and launched a number of startup businesses, where VC and angel investors wanted specifically to hear and see how I navigated risk, failure, and improved based on what was learned. Besides a solid business and/or strategic plan, **resilience** was the underlying characteristic they were looking for. If at first you don't succeed, get back up and try it again!

For me, that valuable experience in for-profit startup over almost two decades has brought about both failure and success. It has allowed me to create capacity to do the things that matter to me and to help others to do the same. And, that experience has been parlayed into nonprofit management, program development and management, social enterprise, strategic planning, grant portfolio management, and the kind of positive social impact that is contextual and measurable.

While many of us are not short on ideas, the most important parts of the process is making space to listen, collaborate, implement, execute, evaluate, learn, modify, and then repeat. We never know how things might unfold in the unpredictable landscape in which we find ourselves these days — a pandemic, systemic racism, political unrest, climate change, unemployment, the availability and affordability of healthcare, equitable access to education, hunger, poverty, and homelessness, and more. The list can go on and on.

*In the unpredictable landscape we navigate today, how will you cultivate **positive social change**? Check out how the **Triad Health Project**, in Greensboro, North Carolina, has been doing it for decades.*

Nevertheless, real change begins with you and me — within each one of us. We have to be willing to step out into the unknown and join with others who are doing the same. Together, we must create the kind of **positive social change** we desire.

Sometimes you just have to Kick Axion®.

Go for it.

Additional Resources

There are a number of additional resources that can assist you in this work. Related to the content of this book, I have pulled together the following short list of books that you will find beneficial as you continue to pull together your strategic plan and financial projections.

Helpful Books to Consider — The following list of book recommendations covers topics highlighted in the book.

- *The Abundant Community: Awakening the Power of Families and Neighborhoods*, by John McKnight and Peter Block (Berret-Koehler Publishers, 2012)

- *The Art of Gathering: How We Meet and Why it Matters*, by Priya Parker (Riverhead Books, 2020)

- *The Art of Social Enterprise: Business as if People Mattered*, by Carl Frankel and Allen Bromberger (New Society Publishers 2013)

- *Business Model Generation: A Handbook for Visionaries, Game Changers, and Challengers*, by Alexander Osterwalder and Yves Pigneur (John Wiley and Sons, 2010)

- *Community: The Structure of Belonging*, by Peter Block (Berret-Koehler Publishers, 2018)

- *Emergent Strategy*, by Adrienne Maree Brown (AK Press, 2017)

- *Harvard Business Review Entrepreneur's Handbook: Everything You Need to Launch and Grow Your New Business*, (Harvard Business Review Press, 2018)

- *Introduction to Social Entrepreneurship*, by Teresa Chahine (CRC Press 2016)

- *The Lean Startup: How Today's Entrepreneurs Use Continuous Innovation to Create Radically Successful Businesses*, by Eric Lies (Currency, 2011)

- *The Social Entrepreneur's Playbook: Pressure Test, Plan, Launch, and Scale Your Enterprise, Expanded Edition*, by Ian C. MacMillan and James D. Thompson (Wharton School Press 2013)

- *Stay Woke: A People's Guide to Making All Black Lives Matter*, by Tehama Lopez Bunyasi and Candis Watts Smith (New York University Press, 2019)

- *Systems Thinking for Social Change: A Practical Guide to Solving Complex Problems, Avoiding Unintended Consequences, and Achieving Lasting Results*, by David Peter Stroh (Chelsea Green Publishers 2015)

- *The Myth of Equality: Uncovering the Roots of Injustice and Privilege*, by Ken Wytsma (IVP Books, 2017)

- *WE Economy: You can find meaning, make a living, and change the world*, by Craig Kielburger, Holly Branson, and Marc Kielburger (Wiley, 2018)

-

About the Authors

Dr. William D. Gibson is a culture geek, innovator, and entrepreneur with 25+ years of blended nonprofit and private sector executive management experience. He is a leader of innovation strategies, social entrepreneurship, and CBO collaboration who is known for solving ambiguous problems at scale.

In the private sector, Gibson spent more than 16 years in business startup and marketing, where his focus was strategy development, corporate communications, product development, and creating a culture where teams could thrive. He has led and collaborated on a number of new startups, supported by more than $5M of VC and angel investor funding and held two design patents. Gibson is also a veteran of the United States Marine Corps.

He completed his doctorate at George Fox University (Portland, OR) focusing on semiotics/future studies, with an emphasis on social and technological advancement. He completed his master's at Duke University (Durham, NC), with a focus on social entrepreneurship. He serves as an adjunct faculty member and dissertation advisor for doctoral candidates at George Fox University. Gibson also serves on the Advisory Board of the Tombolo Institute at Bellevue College for their Customer Experience (CX) Program.

He has presented and consulted internationally in Seoul, Korea; Belfast, Ireland; and London, England, and served in Central America and Japan.

You can reach him at wgibson@sustinerigroup.co.

Dr. LaVerne Lewis is a business navigator, educator, and a global idealist with a passion for making a difference as a change agent. Lewis has 35+ years as a credentialed tax accountant and owns LaVerne Lewis LLC, a full-service accounting-tax-business start-up resource firm including IRS representation. Lewis is Founder/CEO of Women-SEW Global Foundation, a non-profit that empowers women and girls in sewing collectives.

She was appointed by Oregon's Governor Brown to the Board of Directors on TriMet, to serve District 6, which covers East Multnomah County, OR. Dr. Lewis also serves as an elect-Board Member on the Mt. Hood Community College Board of Education and serves as vice president on the NW Faith Foundation Board.

Dr. Lewis holds a doctorate in education from Northcentral University (Prescott, AZ) and a master's in education and human resources from Colorado State University (Ft. Collins, CO). She is currently adjunct faculty in the Business Department at Portland Community College.

Dr. Lewis is passionate about creating positive social change in the lives of women and girls, and works across the globe in raising awareness to achieve economic empowerment. Her 14+ years of global immersion work includes Jordan, Cuba, Brazil, Greece, Tanzania, Morocco, Peru, Costa Rica, Thailand, and China.

You can reach her at llewis@sustinerigroup.co.

Special Thanks

I want to offer a special thank you to Dr. LaVerne Lewis and Patrick Ferguson for editing this book. Their meticulous care was incredibly valuable in completing this final work.

I want to thank Dr. Craig Parrish for his willingness to discuss these ideas and provide me valuable feedback. His healthy skepticism and deep love and hope for community engagement contributed to this final version.

And finally, beyond editing, I want to more directly recognize my partner in crime, Dr. LaVerne Lewis, whose encouragement and early use of this process in the field helped shape this resource. LaVerne, you rock!